Dictionary of
Abbreviations and Acronyms

The **One Hour Wordpower** *series*

One Hour Wordpower

Dictionary of
Abbreviations and
Acronyms

GRAHAM KING

Mandarin
in association with
The Sunday Times

A Mandarin Paperback
DICTIONARY OF ABBREVIATIONS AND ACRONYMS

First published in Great Britain 1994
by Mandarin Paperbacks
an imprint of Reed Consumer Books Ltd
Michelin House, 81 Fulham Road, London SW3 6RB
and Auckland, Melbourne, Singapore and Toronto

A CIP catalogue record for this title
is available from the British Library
ISBN 0 7493 1881 3

Printed and bound in Great Britain
by Cox & Wyman Ltd, Reading, Berkshire

Introduction

Perhaps without our realising it, abbreviations and their smart cousins, acronyms, have become essential elements of our language and lives. We use many of them every day: BBC, BO, DJ, DIY, PDQ. Some of them have been in use for so long we forget the actual words and phrases they represent: RSVP, QED, APC; even a recent invention, AIDS, hides a fearsome medical term a lot of us are already putting out of our minds.

Acronyms – where the initials of a phrase or saying form a meaningful word – are even more pervasive. How many of us would score ten out of ten for reciting correctly the full meanings of ANZAC, AWOL, OXFAM, qango, QANTAS, RADAR, SCUBA, SNAFU, SWALK and WASP? Or even *nimby*, which entered the language only a few years ago? Names of people, too, are abbreviated; you are forgiven if you don't know that RLS is the famous writer Robert Louis Stevenson, but how about GBS, FDR and JFK?

Then of course there are those hundreds of work-horse abbreviations that save us so much time: ft, cm, mph, Herts, hippo, ie, ac, dc, am and so on. No problem here, because we know what they mean and how to use them; but there are hundreds more, those on the fringe of our lives that we see or use only occasionally, that we're not too sure about.

Explaining the meaning of these apparently unintelligible cutdowns is the real purpose of this *Dictionary of Abbreviations and Acronyms* and several thousand of them are listed, mainly those that might cross the paths of the average citizen. There are an estimated half a million abbreviations presently at large around the globe, so it might seem that this collection is but a drop in the ocean. But is your life likely to be ruined by not knowing that AAPP is the

Association of Amusement Park Proprietors, or that the ADMM is the *Association of Dandy Roll and Mould Makers*, or that behind the ABRRM lurks the *Association of British Reclaimed Rubber Manufacturers?* Or, if you are of a bucolic disposition, that **ehm** means *eggs per hen per month*? We think not, but if you disagree, we will happily point you towards the brilliantly exhaustive *Penguin Dictionary of Abbreviations* by Dr John Paxton.

The fact is, many abbreviations break into our lives and then, in time, pass out again, surviving only in erudite dictionaries. Few people in Britain today cannot be unaware of what the letters MGN mean; after the sensational death and business failure of the tycoon Robert Maxwell, Mirror Group Newspapers, or MGN, confronts us in the media day after day. In a decade or two, however, we'll need to look it up.

Meanwhile, it probably pays to know the difference between *et al* and El Al, and you would drop a rather large brick if, at a social gathering, you confused a D & B with a D & C. On the other hand, think of the kudos you'd earn by explaining that FAGS are *Fellows of the American Geographical Society.*

One final point, or period. All the abbreviations in this book are printed without periods. Although this is a widespread trend, and one which avoids typographical fussiness, you should know that the practice is not without its critics.

A

Cryptic Abbreviations

Certain abbreviations are never made public. These are notations that appear on private files, like a doctor's **GOK** on a diagnosis ('*God only knows!*') and a desperate **ADT** on a prescription ('*any damn thing*'). Some health consultants have been known to write **FLK** on a child's interview form, which means '*funny looking kid*'; while **VGLM** is noted down as a tip-off for their colleagues. It means '*very good looking mother*'. Other mystical marks include **CC** (*chief complaint*); **ECU** (*Eternal Care Unit*, ie, *morgue*); **LOL in NAD** (*little old lady in no apparent distress*) and the ghoulish **MFC** (*measure for coffin*).

A	ampere, a unit of electricity.
A1	first class ships in Lloyd's Register.
AA	Anti Aircraft; American Airlines; Alcoholics Anonymous; Automobile Association.
AAA	American Automobile Association.
AAAA	American Association of Advertising Agencies (4As).
AAF	Army Air Force (US).
AAMI	Age Associated Memory Impairment.
AAS	Association of Architects and Surveyors.
AAT	Achievement Anxiety Test.

AATA	Anglo–American Tourist Association.
AAU	Amateur Athletic Union (US); Association of American Universities.
A & N	Army and Navy Stores.
AB	human blood type; able-bodied seaman.
ABA	Amateur Boxing Association; American Bankers' Association; American Bar Association; Antiquarian Booksellers' Association; Association of British Archaeologists.
ABBA	Swedish pop group (Agnetha, Benny, Bjorn, Anni-frid); Amateur Basketball Association.
abbr	abbreviation.
ABC	the alphabet; American Broadcasting Company; Audit Bureau of Circulations; Associated British Cinemas; Australian Broadcasting Commission.
ABCıs, C2s etc	JICNARS (qv) social grading of the National Readership Survey of Britain. A = upper middle class; B = middle class; Cı = lower middle class; C2 = skilled working class; D = working class; E = state pensioners, widows, casual and lowest grade workers.
ABDP	Association of British Directory Publishers.
ABF	Actors' Benevolent Fund; Associated British Foods.
ABLS	Association of British Library Schools.
ABM	Associate in Business Management; anti-ballistic missile.

Abo	Australian Aborigine.
A-bomb	Atomic bomb (originally used on Hiroshima in 1945).
ABPI	Association of the British Pharmaceutical Industry.
ABRACA-DABRA	ABreviations and Related ACronyms Associated with Defense, Astronautics, Business and RAdio-electronics. Name of original listing of abbreviations of space terms (US, 1960s).
ABRS	Association of British Riding Schools.

Acronyms

An abbreviation or an initial becomes an acronym when the letters are pronounceable and the resulting creation is generally accepted into the language. Good recent examples include **RADAR**, **QANTAS**, **WASP**, **SCUBA** and **NIMBY**. Some acronyms, however, are derived from shortened words, like **OXFAM** (*Oxford Committee for Famine Relief*).

ABSA	Association of Business Sponsorship of the Arts.
ABT	Association of Building Technicians.
ABTA	Allied Brewery Traders' Association; Association of British Travel Agents.
a/c	account.
AC	alternating current; appellation contrôlée (quality control of French wines); Arts Council.

ACA	Agricultural Co-operative Association.
ACAS	Advisory, Conciliation and Arbitration Service.
ACC	Army Catering Corps; Association of County Councils.
ACCA	Association of Certified and Corporate Accountants.
ACGB	Arts Council of Great Britain.
ACGBI	Automobile Club of Great Britain and Ireland.
ACORN	A Classification Of Residential Neighbourhoods. A sampling system which divides the country into 38 neighbourhood types, from agricultural villages through inter-war semis to private flats.
ACSN	Association of Collegiate Schools of Nursing.
ACT	Australian Capital Territory; Advisory Council on Technology.
ACTC	Art Class Teacher's Certificate.
ACTT	Association of Cinematograph, Television and Allied Technicians.
ACTU	Australian Council of Trade Unions.
ACU	Auto-Cycle Union.
ACV	actual cash value.
ACW	aircraft(s)woman.
ACWS	aircraft control and warning system.
AD	*anno Domini*: In the year of our Lord, ie, any time after the beginning of the First Century.
ADPSO	Association of Data Processing Service Organisations.
ADRA	Animal Diseases Research Association.
Adv	adverb; advent.

ADCOMSUBORDCOMPHIBSPAC

Supposedly the longest acronym known in English, dating from the 1960s, and short for 'Administrative Command, Amphibious Forces, Pacific Fleet Subordinate Command'. The *Guinness Book of Words* lists a Russian acronym with 54 Cyrillic characters, which itself appears to call for an abbreviation.

AEA	Actors' Equity Association (US).
AEC	Atomic Energy Commission (US).
AEROFLOT	Soviet Air Lines.
AEWHA	All England Women's Hockey Association.
AEWLA	All England Women's Lacrosse Association.
af	as found. Refers to the condition (usually poor) of an item in an auction catalogue.
AFA	Amateur Fencing Association; Amateur Football Association.
AFAM	Ancient Free and Accepted Masons.
AFASIC	Association for All Speech Impaired Children.
AFBS	American and Foreign Bible Society.
AFIA	Apparel and Fashion Industry Association.
AFL	American Football League.
AFL-CIO	American Federation of Labor – Congress of Industrial Organisations.
AFP	*Agence France Presse.*

AFTRA	American Federation of Television and Radio Artists.
Aga	*Aktiebolaget Gas Accumulator*, Swedish oven makers.
AGA	Amateur Gymnastics Association.
AGB	Audits of Great Britain.
AGBI	Artists' General Benevolent Institution.
Agfa	*Aktiengesellschaft fur Anilinfabrikation* (Limited Company for Dye Manufacturing).
AGM	Annual General Meeting; air-to-ground missile.
AGS	American Geographical Society.
AI	artificial intelligence.
AIA	Association of International Accountants.
AIAA	Association of International Advertising Agencies.
AIDAS	Agricultural Industry Development Advisory Service.
AID	artificial insemination by donor.
AIDS	acquired immune deficiency syndrome; aircraft integrated data system.
AILAS	automatic instrument landing approach system.
AIME	American Institute of Mining, Metallurgical and Petroleum Engineers.
AJA	Anglo-Jewish Association; Australian Journalists' Association.
aka	also known as.
AL	American Legion.
ALA	American Library Association.
ALCS	Authors' Licencing and Collecting Society.
ALF	Animal Liberation Front; Automatic Letter Facer.

ALGOL	Algorithmic Language.
ALPA	Airline Pilots' Association.
ALPO	Association of Land and Property Owners.
als	autograph letter, signed.
aM	on the River Main (for certain German cities).
am	*ante meridiem*, or before noon.
AMA	American Medical Association.
AMC	American Motors Corporation; Association of Management Consultants.
AMEX	American Express; American Stock Exchange.

AMIAE, et al

When you see an abbreviation like this beginning with A, it is very likely that the A stands for '*Associate*' – in this case, *Associate Member of the Institute of Automobile Engineers*. There are many hundreds of scientific, professional and trade institutes which issue diplomas of competence; so many, in fact, that it is impossible to list all but the most important in this book.

AMP	Australian Mutual Provident Society.
AMSAM	anti-missile surface-to-air missile.
AMSTRAD	Alan Michael Sugar Trading.
ANC	African National Congress.
anon	anonymous; usually refers to a writer, unknown.

ANZAAS	Australian and New Zealand Association for the Advancement of Science.
ANZAC	Australian and New Zealand Army Corps (WWI).
ANZUS	Australia, New Zealand and US Defence Pact.
AOP	Association of Optical Practitioners.
AP	Associated Press (US).
APEX	Association of Professional, Executive, Clerical and Computer Staff.
aph	aphorism.

Lewd Acronyms

Abbreviations are often used in the cause of euphemism. The socially acceptable word 'pee' derives from the shortened '**p**' for '*piss*'; other contractions include **WC** and **FA** (*sweet FA*), **berk** (*from the Cockney slang, 'Berkshire Hunt'*), **sod** (*from sodomite*), **bumf** (*from bum-fodder*). Acronyms in this class are more elusive, but a well-known favourite is **EDINBURGH**, the meaning of which becomes clearer when it is realised that **BURGH** represents '. . . *Book Usual Room Grand Hotel*'.

APHI	Association of Public Health Inspectors.
APLE	Association of Public Lighting Engineers.
APR	annual percentage rate.

APT	Advance Passenger Train (BR); Automatic Picture Transmission (NASA).
APTIS	all purpose ticket issuing system.
ar, arr	arrive; arrival.
AR	*anno regni* (in the year of the reign); Annual Register; achievement ratio.
ARSR	Air Route Surveillance Radar.
artic	articulated vehicle.
AS	air speed.
ASA	Advertising Standards Authority; Amateur Swimming Association.
asap	as soon as possible.
ASH	Action on Smoking and Health.
ASIO	Australian Security Intelligence Organisation.
ASLEF	Associated Society of Locomotive Engineers and Firemen.
ASM	assistant sergeant-major/sales manager/scoutmaster/stage manager; air-to-surface missile.
ASN	average sample number.
ASO	American Symphony Orchestra.
ASPCA	American Society for the Prevention of Cruelty to Animals.
ASPEP	Association of Scientists and Professional Engineering Personnel.
ASPF	Association of Superannuation and Pension Funds.
ASR	airport surveillance radar.
ATC	air traffic control; Air Training Corps.
ATD	Art Teacher's Diploma; actual time of departure.
ATHE	Association of Teachers in Higher Education.
ATO	assisted take-off.

ATOL	Air Travel Organisers' Licence.
ATS	Auxiliary Territorial Service, precursor of present-day women's army, **WRAC**.
ATV	Associated Television.
AUBTW	Amalgamated Union of Building Trade Workers.
AUEW	Amalgamated Union of Engineering Workers.
AUO	African Unity Organisation.
AUT	Association of University Teachers.
AV	audio-visual.
av	average.
AVR	Army Volunteer Reserve.
AVS	Anti-Vivisection Society.
AWACS	airborne warning and control system.
AWBA	American World's Boxing Association.
AWOL	absent without leave.
AWRE	Atomic Weapons Research Establishment.

B

B	human blood group; 2B, 3B etc., grades of hardness in pencils; lowest note of musical chord.
b	bowled (in cricket).
BA	British Airways; British Academy; British Association.
BAA	British Airports Authority.
BAA & A	British Association of Accountants and Auditors.

BA, BSc, etc.

The original handful of university Bachelor degrees has proliferated to hundreds: **BLE** (*Bachelor of Land Economy*); **BNSc** (*Bachelor of Nursing Science*); **BO** (*Bachelor of Oratory*); **BPd** (*Bachelor of Pedagogy*) and so on. There are dozens of specialist arts degrees: **BA (Arts)**; **BA (Econ)**; **BA (Theol)**, etc.; and a hundred or so species of science degrees: **BSc (H Ec)**; **BSc (Med Lab Tech)** – altogether far too many, unfortunately, to be listed here.

B & B	bed and breakfast.
BAAB	British Amateur Athletics Board.
BAAS	British Association for the Advancement of Science.
Bac	baccalaureat: final French school examination.
BAC	British Aircraft Corporation.
BACO	British Aluminium Company.
BACS	Bankers' Automated Clearing Service.
BADA	British Antique Dealers' Association.
BAe	British Aerospace.
BAEA	British Actors' Equity Association.
BAFTA	British Academy of Film and Television Arts.
BAGA	British Amateur Gymnastics Association.
BAIE	British Association of Industrial Editors.
Ball	Balliol College, Oxford.
BANANA	build absolutely nothing anywhere near anyone.

BAPA	British Airline Pilots' Association.
bar	barometric; barrister; baritone.
BARB	Broadcasters' Audience Research Board.
BARC	British Automobile Racing Club.
Bart's	St Bartholomew's Hospital, London.

BASIC

Acronym for British, American, Scientific, International, Commercial language restricted to a vocabulary of just 850 words. Invented in 1929 by C. K. Ogden and I. A. Richards.

BASIC	Beginners' All-purpose Symbolic Instruction Code.
Bat	battalion; battery.
BAT	British-American Tobacco Company.
BAWA	British Amateur Wrestling Association.
BBBC	British Boxing Board of Control.
BBC	British Broadcasting Corporation.
bbl	barrel; bbls/d = barrels per day.
BBQ	barbecue.
BC	Before Christ; British Council.
bcc	blind carbon copy.
BCCI	Bank of Credit and Commerce.
BE	British Empire.
Beds	Bedfordshire.
BEEB	British Broadcasting Corporation (also **BBC**).
BEF	British Expeditionary Force.
BEM	British Empire Medal.

BENELUX	Customs Union between Belgium, Netherlands and Luxembourg.
Berks	Berkshire.
BFG	big friendly giant.
BFPA	British Film Producers' Association.
BFPO	British Forces Post Office.
bgt	bought.
BHS	British Home Stores; British Horse Society.
BIET	British Institute of Engineering Technology.
BISF	British Iron and Steel Federation.
BIT	binary digit (BInary digiT).
blt; BLT	Built; bacon, lettuce and tomato (sandwich).
blvd	*boulevarde.*
BMJ	*British Medical Journal.*
BMT	British Mean Time.
BMTA	British Motor Trade Association.
BMW	*Bayerische Motoren Werke*, Bavaria.
BMX	bicycle motorcross.
bn	billion.
BNA	British Nursing Association.
bo	body odour; box office.
Bod	Bodleian Library, Oxford.
BOLTOP	Better on lips than on paper (placed below a paper kiss – X – on a lover's envelope).
BOOK	box of organised knowledge (definition of a book, coined by Anthony Burgess).
BOP	*Boy's Own Paper* (1879–1967).
BOSS	Bureau of State Security (South Africa).
bot	botany; bottle; bottom.
BPA	British Philatelic Association.
BPC	British Pharmaceutical Code; British Printing Corporation.

BPS	British Pharmacological Society.
br	branch; bridge; brown.
BR	British Rail.
bra	brassière.
BRM	British Racing Motors.
bro	brother.
BSC	British Safety Council; British Steel Corporation; British Sugar Corporation.
BSCP	British Standard Code of Practice.
BSE	bovine spongiform encephalopathy ('mad cow' disease).
BSG	British Standard Gauge (railways).
BSI	British Standards Institution.
BSRA	British Sound Recording Association.
Bt, Bart	Baronet.
BTC	British Transport Commission.
btl	bottle.
BTU	British thermal unit.
Bucks	Buckinghamshire.
BUPA	British United Provident Association.
bur	bureau; buried.
BURMA	be undressed ready, my angel.
BV	*Besloten Vennootschap* (Dutch private company).
BVD's	mens' one-piece underwear, originally made by the US firm Bradley, Voorhees & Day.
BVI	British Virgin Islands.
b/w	black and white; monochrome.
BWA	British West Africa.
BWIA	British West Indies Airways.
BWV	*Bach Werke-Verzeichnis* (catalogue of the works of Bach).
BYO	bring your own.

C

Cabal

The story goes that the word **cabal** (a secret clique) derives from an acronym made up of the first letters of the names of five ministers of Charles II who signed an infamous treaty in 1672 – Clifford, Ashley Cooper, Buckingham, Arlington and Lauderdale. A good story, but not true; that the initials form the word is coincidental. Cabal comes from the Hebrew **qabbala**, meaning 'secret doctrines'.

C	degree of heat in Celsius or centigrade; 100 in Roman numerals.
c	cent; cape; carat; century; central; approximately, caught (in cricket); catcher (in baseball).
©	copyright.
Ca; CA	California; Canada.
cab	taxi (from *cabriolet*).
CAB	Citizens' Advice Bureau.
cal	calibre; calorie.
CALTEX	California Texas Petroleum Corporation.
Camb	Cambrian; Cambridge.
Cambs	Cambridgeshire.
CAMRA	Campaign for Real Ale.
canc	cancelled; cancellation.

C & A	Chain of stores named after Dutch brothers Clemens and Auguste Breeninkmeyer.
Cant	Canterbury.
Cantab	Cambridge (from *Cantabrigia*).
CAP	Common Agricultural Policy (EU).
cap	capital city; capacity; capital letter; captain.
carr	carriage.
CAT	Computer Assisted Translation/ Typesetting.
cat	catalogue.
CATscan	computerised axial tomography.
CATV	cable/community antenna television.
CB	Citizens' Band (radio frequencies).
CBC	Canadian Broadcasting Corporation.
CBI	Confederation of British Industries.
cbk	cheque-book.
CBS	Colombia Broadcasting System.
CBSO	City of Birmingham Symphony Orchestra.
cc	carbon copy; cubic centimetre.
CC	Cricket/Croquet/Cruising/Cycling Club.
c & c	curtains and carpets.
CCC	Central Criminal Court (Old Bailey, London).
CCCP	Union of Soviet Socialist Republics.
CCP	Chinese Communist Party.
CCTV	closed circuit television.
cd fwd	carried forward.
CDS	Civil Defence Services.
CETEX	Committee on Extra-Terrestrial Exploration.

The Chemical Elements

Ac	actinium	Au	gold	Pm	promethium
Al	aluminium	Hf	hafnium	Pa	protoactinium
Am	americium	He	helium	Ra	radium
Sb	antimony	Ho	holmium	Rn	radon
Ar	argon	H	hydrogen	Re	rhenium
As	arsenic	In	indium	Rh	rhodium
At	astatine	I	iodine	Rb	rubidium
Ba	barium	Ir	iridium	Ru	ruthenium
Bk	berkelium	Fe	iron	Sm	samarium
Be	beryllium	Kr	krypton	Sc	scandium
Bi	bismuth	La	lanthanum	Se	selenium
B	boron	Lr	lawrencium	Si	silicon
Br	bromine	Pb	lead	Ag	silver
Cd	cadmium	Li	lithium	Na	sodium
Cs	caesium	Lu	lutetium	Sr	strontium
Ca	calcium	Mg	magnesium	S	sulphur
Cf	californium	Mn	manganese	Ta	tantalum
C	carbon	Md	mendelevium	Tc	technetium
Ce	cerium	Hg	mercury	Te	tellurium
Cl	chlorine	Mo	molybdenum	Tb	terbium
Cr	chromium	Nd	neodymium	Tl	thallium
Co	cobalt	Ne	neon	Th	thorium
Cb	columbium	Np	neptunium	Tm	thulium
Cu	copper	Ni	nickel	Sn	tin
Cm	curium	Nb	niobium	Ti	titanium
Dy	dysprosium	N	nitrogen	W	tungsten
Es	einsteinium	Os	osmium	U	uranium
Er	erbium	O	oxygen	V	vanadium
Eu	europium	Pd	palladium	Xe	xenon
Fm	fermium	P	phosphorous	Yb	ytterbium
F	fluorine	Pt	platinum	Y	yttrium
Fr	francium	Pu	plutonium	Zn	zinc
Gd	gadolinium	Po	polonium	Zr	zirconium
Ga	gallium	K	potassium		
Ge	germanium	Pr	praseodymium		

cf	compare; calf (in bookbinding); centre forward (football); centre fielder (baseball).
CFC	chlorofluorocarbons.
cfi	cost, freight & insurance.
cg	centigram; centre of gravity.
CGA	Country Gentlemen's Association.
cgt	capital gains tax.
ch	chain; chapter; chairman (*also* **Chm**).
Chi	Chicago.
chron	chronological.
Chunder	watch under!
CI	Channel Islands.
CIA	Central Intelligence Agency (of the US).
CIB	Criminal Investigation Branch.
CID	Criminal Investigation Department.
Cie	Company (as in *& Cie*, in France).
C-in-C	Commander-in-Chief.
CIP	Common Industrial Policy.
circ	circulation (of publications); circular.
CJD	Creutzfeldt-Jacob disease.
cl	centilitre; class; cloth (in bookbinding).
Cllr	Councillor.
clr	clear.
cm	centimetre; cm^2 = square cm; cm^3 = cubic cm.
Cmdr	Commander.
Cmdre	Commodore.
CND	Campaign for Nuclear Disarmament.
CNR	Canadian National Railway.
cnr	corner.
c/o	in the care of; cash order.

Co	Company; county.
CO	Commanding Officer; Central Office.
cob	close of business.
COBOL	Computer Business Oriented Language.
COD	cash/collect on delivery.
CODOT	Classification of Occupations and Directory of Occupational Titles (Dept of Employment).
COED	computer operated electronic display; *Concise Oxford English Dictionary*.
co-ed	co-educational.
C of A	Certificate of Airworthiness.
C of E	Church of England.
COI	Central Office of Information.
coll	collection; college; colloquialism.
COMECON	Council for Mutual Economic Assistance (EU).
COMPAC	Commonwealth Trans-Pacific Telephone Cable.
conc	concentrated.
cond	condition; conduct.
CONSOLS	Consolidated Annuities (Government securities).
cont	continued.
Co-Op	Co-operative Society or Union.
CORE	Congress of Racial Equality (US).
corp	corporation.
corr	correction.
CO₂	carbon dioxide gas.
cp	compare.
CPA	Canadian Pacific Airlines.
Cpl	Corporal.
CPRE	Council for the Protection of Rural England.
CPRW	Council for the Protection of Rural Wales.

An Abbreviation too Far?

What the advertiser was really seeking were trainees for insurance analysis!

CRAFT Club	'Can't Remember A Flippin' Thing' Club.
CRE	Commission for Racial Equality.
Cres	Crescent.
CRO	Criminal Records Office.
CSA	Child Support Agency.
CSE	Certificate of Secondary Education.
CSI	Chartered Surveyors' Institution.
CSO	Central Statistical Office.
Ct	Carat, unit of weight for precious stones and pearls. *See also* **Kt** (karat).
CTC	Carbon tetrachloride (fire retardant).
CTN	Confectioner, tobacconist and newsagent.
CTO	cancelled to order (philately).
cu cm	cubic centimetre (*also* **cu in** = cubic inch).
CUNY	City University of New York.
CUP	Cambridge University Press.
CURE	Care, Understanding, Research organisation for the welfarE of drug addicts.
cv	*curriculum vitae*: a summary of one's career in life.

C & W	Country & Western (music).
CWA	Civil Works Administration (US); Country Women's Association (Australia).
CWL	Catholic Women's League.
cwo	cash with order.
cwt	hundredweight (112 lbs).
cyl	cylinder.
Cz	Czechoslovakia.

D

d	old pence (½d, 2d, 9d, etc.).
D	Roman numeral for 500; Democrat (US); *Deus* = God; *dominus* = Lord.
DA	District Attorney (US).
DAD	Deputy Assistant Director.
Dan-Air	Davies and Newman Ltd (British airline).
DAR	Daughters of the American Republic.
DAT	Digital Analogue Technology.
DATA	Draughtsmen's and Allied Technicians' Association.
dB	Decibel.
D & B	Dun & Bradstreet (financial reports).
DC	District of Colombia (US, as in Washington DC); death certificate.
dc	direct current.
DC3	Douglas Aircraft, Type 3 (also **DC4, DC6, DC9** etc.).

DCA	Department of Civil Aviation (Australia).
DCM	Distinguished Conduct Medal.
D and C	dilation and curettage (uterus operation).
d col	double column (publishing).
DD	direct debit.
d and d	drunk and disorderly.
DDA	Disabled Drivers' Association.
D Day	Start of Allied invasion of Europe, WW2.
DDG	Deputy Director General.
DDS	Dewey Decimal System (library classification).
DDT	dichloro-diphenyl-trichloroethane (insecticide).
dec	deceased; decimal; decrease.
Dec	December.
DJ	Disc Jockey (also DeeJay); dinner jacket.
def	definition; definitive; defect; deficit.
del	*delineavit* = drawn by (on engravings).
deli	delicatessen.
DELTA	Don't Expect Luggage To Arrive (a friendly poke at US Delta Airlines).
demo	demonstration.
dep	depart; departure; depot; deposit.
DEP	Department of Employment and Productivity.
Dept	Department.
DERV	Diesel Engined Road Vehicle.
DES	Department of Education and Science.
det	detached.
Det	Detective.
DEWLINE	Distant Early Warning Viewing Line.

DFC	Distinguished Flying Cross.
DFM	Distinguished Flying Medal.
D-G	Director General.
DHA	District Health Authority.
DHSS	Department of Health and Social Security, formerly. (Now split into **DoH** and **DSS**).
diag	diagonal.
diam	diameter.
DIC	Drunk in Charge (Police term).
dil	dilute.
DINKY	Double Income, No Kids Yet.
divn	division.
DIY	do-it-yourself.
DLO	Dead Letter Office.
Dlr	Dealer.
DM	*Deutsche Mark* (German currency unit).
DMS	Data Management System.
DMZ	Demilitarised Zone.
DNA	deoxyribonucleic acid.
D NOTICE	Restriction warning on security information.
DOA	dead on arrival.
DOM	*Deó Optimo Maximo*. Latin for 'God is best and greatest', the motto of the Benedictine order and seen on the labels of Benedictine liqueur; Dirty Old Man.
DORA	Defence of the Realm Act, enacted during the 1914–18 war to enforce security restrictions.
dorm	dormitory.
doz	dozen.
DPM	Deputy Prime Minister.
DPP	Director of Public Prosecutions.
dr	debit; debtor; drachm; drachma; drawn.
Dr	Doctor.

29

Dip Ed

This is the abbreviation for *Diploma of Education*, and there are many more, like **Dip Mech E** (*Diploma of Mechanical Engineering*) and **Dip Orth** (*Diploma of Orthodontics*). Invariably, **Dip = Diploma**, which is sometimes shortened to **D**.

DSC	Distinguished Service Cross.
DSM	Distinguished Service Medal.
DSO	Distinguished Service Order.
DST	Daylight Saving Time.
dstn	destination.
DTI	Department of Trade and Industry.
dub	dubious.
dup	duplicate.
DV	Domestic Violence Division, Scotland Yard.
DVLC	Driver and Vehicle Licencing Centre, Swansea.
d/w	dust wrapper (books).
D/W	deadweight.
DWI	Dutch West Indies.
dwt	pennyweight.
DX	Deep Six; to 'deep six' it = bury it, abandon it.
DYB	Do Your Best! (Boy Scout motto).

E

E; e	East, eastern; energy; evening.
ea	each.
E and OE	errors and omissions excepted.
EAT	earliest arrival time.
EBA	English Bowling Association.
EBC	European Billiards Confederation.
EBL	European Bridge League.
EBU	European Boxing Union; European Badminton Union; European Broadcasting Union; English Bridge Union.
EC	European Community (*see* **EEC** and **EU**).
ECD	early closing day.
ECG	electrocardiogram.
ECM	European Common Market (*see* **EEC** and **EU**).
ECSC	European Coal and Steel Community.
ecu	European currency unit (equivalent to US $1).
ECU	English Church Union; extra close-up.
ed	editor; edition.
Edin	Edinburgh.
EDSAT	Educational Television Satellite.
EDT	Eastern Daylight Time.
EEC	European Economic Community (*see* **EU**).
EEG	electroencephalograph.
EENT	Eye, Ear, Nose and Throat (medical specialism).
EET	Eastern European Time.
EFTA	European Free Trade Association.

eg	*exempligratia* = for example.
EGM	Extraordinary General Meeting.
EGU	English Golf Union.
EGYPT	Eager to grab your pretty tits.
EHF	European Hockey Federation.
EL	Easy Listening (radio music).
el	electrical; elevated railway (US).
El Al	Israeli Airlines.
elev	elevation.
ELF	Eritrean Liberation Front.
ELT	English Language Teaching.
ELU	English Lacrosse Union.
E-mail	Electronic mail.
emer	emergency; emeritus.
EMI	Electric and Musical Industries Limited.
Emp	Emperor; Empress; Empire.
EMS	European Monetary System.
EMU	European Monetary Unit.
encyc	encyclopedia.

Points of the Compass

Starting with *north* and moving clockwise: **N** (*north*) **NNE** (*north-north-east*) **NE** (*north-east*) **ENE** (*east-north-east*) **E** (*east*) **ESE** (*east-south-east*) **SE** (*south-east*) **SSE** (*south-south-east*) **S** (*south*) **SSW** (*south-south-west*) **SW** (*south-west*) **WSW** (*west-south-west*) **W** (*west*) **WNW** (*west-north-west*) **NW** (*north-west*) **NNW** (*north-north-west*).

eng	engine; engineer.
Eng	England.
engr	engraver; engraved.
ENO	English National Opera.

ENT	Ear, Nose and Throat (*see* **EENT**).
env	envelope.
EOC	Equal Opportunities Commission.
EOKA	Cypriot Campaign for Union with Greece.
EPCOT	Experimental Prototype Community of Tomorrow (at Disney World, Florida).

E-Numbers

These are code numbers for approved natural and artificial additives to food and drink, mandatory on all EU product labelling since 1986. Natural additives include **E150** (*caramel*), **E270** (*lactic acid*) and the emulsifying and stabilising group: **E406** (*agar*), **E412** (*guar gum*) and **E440** (*pectin*). **E300**, **301**, **302**, **307** and **322** are antioxidants. The range **E210–227** are *benzoic, sulphur* and *sulphite preservatives*, while **E249–252** include the more controversial nitrites and nitrates found in cooked and cured meats. Even more controversial are the colours, **E160** (*used in cheese*), **E104** (*used to colour smoked fish*) and especially the notorious **E102**, or *Tantrazine*, used to heighten the orange colour of drinks and which, according to a newspaper report, 'can bring them [hyperactive children] out in a rash or drive them barmy'.

EPNS	electroplated nickel silver.
EPOCH	End Physical Punishment of Children.
EPOS	Electronic Point of Sale.
eps	earnings per share.
equiv	equivalent.

ER	*Elisabeth Regina* = Queen Elizabeth.
ERBM	Extended Range Ballistic Missile.
ERG	electrical resistance gauge.
ERGOM	European Research Group on Management.
ERM	Exchange Rate Mechanism.

European Car Registration Letters

The letters GB, IRL, F and NL on motor vehicles are commonly seen and most of us know that they identify the country of registration: Great Britain, Ireland, France and Holland. But what of GBG or E? Here's an identification list of European vehicle registration letters:

Al Albania **GBA** Alderney **AND** Andorra **A** Austria **B** Belgium **BG** Bulgaria **CS** former Czechoslovakia **CY** Cyprus **DK** Denmark **FR** Faroe Islands **SF** Finland **F** France **D** Germany **GBZ** Gibraltar **GB** Great Britain **GR** Greece **GBG** Guernsey **H** Hungary **IS** Iceland **IRL** Ireland **GBM** Isle of Man **I** Italy **GBJ** Jersey **FL** Liechtenstein **L** Luxembourg **M** Malta **MC** Monaco **NL** Netherlands **N** Norway **PL** Poland **P** Portugal **RO** Romania **RSM** San Marino **E** Spain **S** Sweden **CH** Switzerland **V** Vatican City **YU** former Yugoslavia

ERNIE	Electronic Random Number Indicator Equipment.
ERU	English Rugby Union.
ERV	English Revised Version of the Bible.
ESA	Educational Supply Association.

ESCAP	Economic and Social Commission for Asia and the Pacific.
ESCO	Educational, Scientific and Cultural Organisation.
ESG	English Standard Gauge.
ESL	English as a Second Language.
ESN	educationally subnormal.
esp	especially.
ESP	extra-sensory perception; English for Special Purposes.
Es	Esquire.
ESSO	Standard Oil Company.
est	established; estate.
EST	Eastern Standard Time; earliest start time.
ESU	English Speaking Union.
ETA	estimated time of arrival.
et al	*et alii* = and others; *et alibi* = and elsewhere.
etc	*et cetera* = and so on.
ETD	estimated time of departure.
EU	Evangelical Union; European Union.
Euro$	Eurodollar.
EVA	Extra Vehicular Activity (outside a spacecraft).
evg	evening (*also* **evng**).
ex	excellent; excess; excursion; exempt.
exag	exaggerate.
exch	exchange.
excl	exclude; exclusive.
exec	executive.
exes	expenses.
exhib	exhibit; exhibitor.
exp	expense; experience; experiment; export; express.
EXPO	large-scale exposition or exhibition.
expurg	expurgate.
ext	extension; exterior; external.

F

F, f	Fail (in examinations); fog; fine; farad (electrical unit); Fahrenheit (degrees of heat); fast; firm; founded; franc; Friday.
FA	Football Association; family allowance.

F I Mech E

Fellow of the Institute of Mechanical Engineers. There are millions of Fellows belonging to hundreds of Institutes – F Inst P C, for example, is a Fellow of the Institute of Public Cleansing – so when you see an abbreviation beginning with **F**, or **FI**, there is a good chance it refers to a Fellow of some learned, professional or trade body. But you can be fooled. There are a lot of FIs which are abbreviations of the French *Fédération Internationale*, such as **FIFA**, which is the International Association Football Federation. Other traps include **FID** (Falkland Island Dependencies), **FICA** (Federal Insurance Contributions Act – US), **FIFO** (first in, first out), **FEA** (Federation of European Aerosol Associations), **FGA** (Flat Glass Association), and **FPA** (Family Planning Association). And take care if a name has the attachment **FRCS**; it could be that the holder is an esteemed Fellow of the Royal College of Surgeons or, on the other hand, a member of the Federation of Rabbit Clearance Societies. Alas, only the most important can be listed here.

FAA	Federal Aviation Administration (US); Fleet Air Arm.
facs	facsimile.
Fahr	Fahrenheit (degrees of heat).
fam	familiar; family.
f & a	fore and aft.
f & d	freight and demurrage.
f & f	fixtures and fittings.
f & t	fire and theft.
FAO	Food and Agriculture Organisation (of the UN).
fao	finished all over.
faq	fair average quality.
FAX	Facsimile electronic transceiving equipment.
FC	Forestry Commission.
fcap	foolscap.
fcg	facing (as in fcg page).
FCI	International Federation of Kennel Clubs.
FCO	Foreign and Commonwealth Office.
fd	forward; found; founded.
FDA	Food and Drug Administration (US).
FDC	First Day Cover (in philately).
Fdr	Founder.
FDR	Franklin Delano Roosevelt, former US President.
Feb	February.
fec	*fecit* = made by (seen on prints and engravings).
Fed	Federal; Federal Reserve Bank (US).
fem	female; feminine.
FES	foil, épée and sabre.
Fest	Festival.
ff	fixed focus.
FF	Fianna Fáil (Irish political party).

FG	Fine Gael (Irish political party).
F/H	Freehold (*also* **fhold** *and* **fhld** *and* **frld**).
FHA	Federal Housing Administration (US).
FIAT	*Fabbrica Italiana Automobili Torino*, Turin car makers.
fict	fiction (also fic).
FICA	Federal Insurance Contributions Act (US).
FIFA	International Association Football Federation; International Federation of Art Film-makers.
fig	figure.
FIH	International Hockey Federation.
FILO	first in, last out.
FIM	French International Federation of Musicians; International Motorcycle Federation.
fin	*finis* = the end.
fina	following items not available.
FINA	International Amateur Swimming Federation.
Findus	Fruit INDUStries Ltd.
fix	fixture.
Flak	*Fliegerabwehrkanone*, or anti-aircraft gun. The term flak was used to describe the shellbursts.
fld	filed.
fldg	folding.
FLN	*Front de Libération Nationale*, or National Liberation Front of Algeria.
fl oz	fluid ounce.
flrg	flooring.
flt	flight; *also* as in Flt Lieutenant.
fm	farm; frequency modulation.
FMCG	Fast Moving Consumer Goods.
fmr	former.

38

FO	Foreign Office; Flying Officer (*also* **F/O**).
FOC; foc	Father of the Chapel (in print union); free of charge.
fo'c's'le	forecastle.
FOH	Front of House.
fol	folio; following.
FOOTSIE	*see* **FT-SE 100 Index**.
FOREST	Freedom Organisation for the Right to Enjoy Smoking Tobacco.
FORTRAN	Formula translation (computer language).
4WD	four-wheel drive.
fp	fireplace; fresh paragraph; fully paid.
FPA	Family Planning Association.
FPO	Field Post Office.
fps	feet/frames per second.
FPS	Fellow of the Pharmaceutical/ Philosophical/Physical Society.
fr	front; from; frequent; fruit; father; franc.
FRAME	Fund for the Replacement of Animals in Medical Experiments.
FRED	Fast Reactor Experiment, Dounreay, Scotland.
Fri	Friday.
front	frontispiece (*also* **frontis**).
FT	*Financial Times*, London.
ft	foot; feet (**sq ft** = square ft; **cu ft** = cubic ft).
FTC	Federal Trade Commission (US).
ftg	fitting.
FT (Index)	*Financial Times* Industrial Ordinary Share Index.
FT-SE 100 Index	*Financial Times* Stock Exchange 100-Share Index (**FOOTSIE**).
FU	Farmers' Union.
fur	furlong.

fut	future.
FWA	Federal Works Agency (US).
fwd	forward.
FWT	fair wear and tear.
fyi	for your information.

ABQUIZ

Although all the abbreviations in this book are spelled without periods, their meanings are invariably clear. Confusion arises, however, when necessary spacing between the elements of an abbreviation is also banished. For example:

1. **POBOX** 2. **VOLIV** 3. **FLOZ**
4. **PROMOMA** 5. **DOOGO**

Written out in full these are:

1. P.O. Box 2. Volume 4 3. Fluid ounces
4. Public Relations Officer, Museum of Modern Art 5. Director of Operations, Orbiting Geophysical Observatory (US).

G

g	gallon; gram; gravity.
GA	Geologists' Association; Geographical Association.
Gabba	Wollongabba (Queensland Cricket Club ground in Brisbane).

g/a	general average.
Gael	Gaelic.
G & T	gin and tonic.
gal	gallon (*also* **gall**).
GALAXY	General Automatic Luminosity high-speed scanner at Royal Observatory, Edinburgh.
gall	gallery.
GAP	Great American Public.
GARP	Global Atmospheric Research Programme.
GASP	Group Against Smog Pollution.
GATT	General Agreement on Tariffs & Trade.

GAY

An abbreviation or a purloined adjective? Whatever the truth, here's a word that's acquired a considerable mythology in just a couple of decades. There's a strong claim that the word's use as a description for a homosexual person derives from New York's 1969 Stonewall rally during which banners proclaimed that the marchers were 'Good As You'. On the other hand, usage of the word **gay** in this context can be traced to late nineteenth-century literature, although it did not become popular until the 1960s. Incidentally, gay in a former usage (gay blade, gay dog) is now politically incorrect because it is sexist; whereas **gay** (**gay man**, **gay woman**) is not.

GAYE	Give As You Earn (scheme to deduct charitable contributions from employees' pay packets).

gaz	gazetted; gazetteer.
GB	Great Britain (England, Scotland and Wales).
GBE	Grand Cross Order of the British Empire.
GBH	Grievous Bodily Harm.
GBS	Dramatist George Bernard Shaw.
GC	George Cross, ribboned medal for gallantry.
GCB	Knight Grand Cross of the Most Honourable Order of the Bath.
GCE	General Certificate of Education.
GCHQ	Government Communications Headquarters.
GCM	Good Conduct Medal; General Court Martial.
GCMG	Knight Grand Cross of the Most Distinguished Order of St Michael and St George.
GCSE	General Certificate of Secondary Education.
GCVO	Grand Cross of the Royal Victorian Order.
gd	good.
GDBA	Guide Dogs for the Blind Association.
gdn	garden.
GDR	German Democratic Republic (formerly E Germany).
GE	General Electric.
ge	gilt edge (books).
GEC	General Electric Corporation.
GEMS	Global Environmental Monitoring System.
gen	gender; general; generic; genuine.
gent	Gentleman, *also* **Gents** = gentlemen.
GEOREF	International Geographic Reference System.

GESTAPO	*GEheime STAats-POlizei*, former German secret police.
GF	General Foods Ltd.
GFR	German Federal Republic (formerly W Germany).
GFS	Girls' Friendly Society.
GG	Grenadier Guards.
GGA	Girl Guides Association.
GHQ	General Headquarters.
GHS	Girls' High School.
gi	galvanised iron.
GI	Government Issue (Term for US soldier).
Gib	Gibraltar.
GIGO	garbage in, garbage out (computer term).
GKN	Guest, Keen & Nettlefolds (engineering co.).
gl	glass; gill.
Glad	(*also* **gladdie**) Gladiolus; also Gladys Moncrieff, former Australian singer (d. 1976) known as 'Our Glad'.
Glam	Glamorganshire.
GLASS	Gay, Lesbian Assembly for Student Support (US).
GLC	Greater London Council.
gld	guilder, Dutch monetary unit (*also* **Gldr**).
GLOMEX	Global Oceanographic and Meteorological Experiment.
Glos	Gloucester; Gloucestershire.
GM	General Motors Corporation; George Medal, awarded for acts of bravery.
gm	gram.
G-Man	Officer of the US Federal Bureau of Investigation (Government man).

GMB	Grand Master of the Order of the Bath.
GMBE	Grand Master of the Order of the British Empire.
GmbH	*Gesellschaft mit beschrankter Haftung*, a German limited liability company.
GMC	General Medical Council.
GMT	Greenwich Mean Time; Greenwich Meridian Time.
gn	guinea (formerly £1.05).
gnd	ground.
GNP	Gross National Product.
GOM	Grand Old Man (originally Prime Minister Gladstone).
GOP	Grand Old Party (the US Republican Party); *Girls' Own Paper* (1880–1956).
Gov	Governor.
Gov-Gen	Governor-General.
govt	government.
GP	general practitioner (medical doctor); Grand Prix; general purpose.
Gp Capt	Group Captain.
G Ph	Graduate in Pharmacy.
gph	gallons per hour.
GPI	general paralysis of the insane.
GPO	General Post Office.
GQ	General Quarters.
gr	grain; gram; gross; grand; group; grade.
GRA	Greyhound Racing Association.
grad	graduate; gradient.
GRI	*Georgius Rex Imperator* = George, King and Emperor.
grm	gram
GS	Geological Survey; gold standard.
GSM	general sales manager.

44

GSO	General Staff Officer.				
G-Spot	Grafenberg Spot (vaginal erogenous zone).				
gtd	guaranteed.				
gte	gilt top edge (books).				
guar	guaranteed.				
GUM	*Gosudarstvenni Universalni Magazin* (official Russian department store).				
GUS	Great Universal Stores (GB).				

American States

Although some states do not have designated abbreviations (Idaho, Ohio, etc.), most do:

Ala	Alabama	**Ariz**	Arizona	**Ark**	Arkansas
Ca	California	**Co**	Colorado	**Ct**	Connecticut
Del	Delaware·	**Fla**	Florida	**Ga**	Georgia
Ill	Illinois	**Ind**	Indiana	**Kans**	Kansas
Ky	Kentucky	**La**	Louisiana	**Md**	Maryland
Mass	Massachusetts	**Me**	Maine	**Mich**	Michigan
Minn	Minnesota	**Miss**	Mississippi	**Mo**	Missouri
Mont	Montana	**Nebr**	Nebraska	**Nev**	Nevada
NH	New Hampshire	**NJ**	New Jersey	**NMex**	New Mexico
NY	New York	**NC**	North Carolina	**NDak**	North Dakota
Okla	Oklahoma	**Or**	Oregon	**Pa**	Pennsylvania
PR	Puerto Rico	**RI**	Rhode Is	**SC**	South Carolina
SDak	South Dakota	**Tenn**	Tennessee	**Tex**	Texas
Vt	Vermont	**Va**	Virginia	**VI**	Virgin Islands
Wa	Washington	**WVa**	West Virginia		
Wyo	Wyoming	**DS**	Washington, District of Colombia		

guv	guv'nor, governor. Cockney term which recognises that 'you're the boss'.
GV	*Grande Vitesse* (fast French train).
gvt	government.
GWP	Government White Paper.
GWR	Great Western Railway (former).
gym	gymnasium; gymnastics.

H

H	degree of hardness in pencils – 2H, 3H etc.
h	hardness; heavy, hour; horizontal; height.
ha	hectare.
hab	habitat; habitation.
Hak Soc	Hakluyt Society.
h & t	hardened and tempered.
H & W	Harland & Wolff, Belfast shipbuilding yard.
hanky	handkerchief (*also* **hankie**).
ha'penny	halfpenny (ha'p'orth = halfpenny worth).
HAS	Health Advisory Service.
haz	hazard; hazardous.
HB	hard black pencil.
hbk	hardback book.
H-bomb	Hydrogen bomb.
hbr	harbour.
HC	Headmasters' Conference; High Commissioner; health certificate; High Court; highly commended; *hors concours* = not for competition; Hague Convention; house of correction.

Hcap	handicap (*also* **hcp**).
HCB	House of Commons Bill.
HCSA	Hospital Consultants' and Specialists' Association.
HCVC	Historic Commercial Vehicle Club.
hcw	hot and cold water (*also* **h & c; hc**).
hdbk	hardback book; handbook.
hdg	heading.
H Dip Ed	Higher Diploma in Education.
hdle	hurdle.
hdlg	handling (**hdlg chg** = handling charge).
hdqrs	headquarters.
HDV	heavy duty vehicle.
H & E	*Health & Efficiency* naturist journal; heredity and environment.
Heb	Hebrew; Hebraic.
HEC	Health Education Council.
HECTOR	Heated Experimental Carbon Thermal Oscillator Reactor.
hem	haemoglobin; haemorrhage.
Her	Herefordshire.
HERALD	Highly Enriched Reactor at Aldermaston, Berks.
herb	herbarium; herbalist; herbaceous.
HERMES	Heavy Element and Radioactive Material Electromagnetic Separator.
HERO	Hot Experimental Reactor O-power.
Herts	Hertfordshire.
HET	Heavy Equipment Transporter.
hex	hexagonal.
HF	hard firm pencil.
hf	half (**hf cf** = half calf binding).
hgr	hangar.
hgt	height.
HGV	heavy goods vehicle.

hh	hands (height measurement of horses).
HH	His Holiness; His (or Her) Honour; heavy hydrogen.
Hib	Hibernian.
hi fi	high fidelity.
HI	Her/His Imperial Majesty.
Hind	Hindi; Hindu.
hippo	hippopotamus.
hist	historic; historian.
histol	histology; histologist.
HIV	Human Immunodeficiency Syndrome.
HIV-P	Human Immunodeficiency Syndrome – Positive.
HK	Hong Kong.
HM	Her/His Majesty; harbour master.
hm	headmaster; headmistress.
HMAS	Her Majesty's Australian Ship.
HMC	Headmasters' Conference (also HC).
HMHS	Her Majesty's Hospital Ship.
HMIS	Her Majesty's Inspector of Schools.
HMIT	Her Majesty's Inspector of Taxes.
HMP	Her Majesty's Prison.
HMS	Her Majesty's Ship.
HMSO	Her Majesty's Stationery Office.
HMV	His Master's Voice.
Hnrs	Honours.
ho	house.
HO	head office; Home Office.
hoc	held on charge.
HoC	House of Commons (*also* **H of C**; **HOC**).
HoD	head of department.
HoL	House of Lords (*also* **H of L**).
hol	holiday (**hols** = holidays).
Holl	Holland.
HOLLAND	Hope Our Love Lasts, Lives, And Never Dies.

homeo	homeopathic.
homo	homosexual.
Hon	Honorary (ie, **Hon Sec** = Honorary Secretary); Honourable (ie, the Hon Matilda Smythe).

Honorary Fellows

You would expect the abbreviation for an Honorary Fellow of the Society of Engineers to be HFSE – but no! The correct abbreviation discards the prefix H, and it is simply FSE. Likewise with most other societies and institutes. But watch for the odd exception, like HROI, who is an Honorary Member of the Royal Institute of Oil Painters.

---

hons	honours.
HOPEFUL	Hard-up Old Person Expecting Full Useful Life.
horol	horology; horologist.
hort	horticulture; horticulturalist.
hosp	hospital.
HOTOL	HOrizontal Take Off and Landing aircraft.
hp	horse power; hire purchase.
HP	Houses of Parliament; hot pressed (paper).
HP Sauce	Houses of Parliament Sauce.
HPTA	Hire Purchase Trade Association.
HQ	headquarters.
HR	House of Representatives (US); Home Rule.
HRH	Her/His Royal Highness.
Hrn	*Herren* (German: Gentlemen).

HRT	hormone replacement therapy.
H Sch	high school.
hse	house (*also* **hsekpr** = housekeeper).
HSV	herpes simplex virus.
ht	height; heat; high tension; half time.
h/t	halftone.
htd	heated.
ht wkt	hit wicket (in cricket).
Hub	Not an abbreviation, but a nickname for Boston, USA.
Hum	humanities; human; humorous.
HVA	Health Visitors' Association.
hvy	heavy.
h/w	husband and wife; hot water.
HWLB	high water, London Bridge.
HWM	high water mark.
HWS	hot water system.
hwy	highway.
hyb	hybrid.

FOOTNOTES

Here are the meanings of some of those italicised footnote abbreviations put there to puzzle us: **abr** = *abridged*, **app** = *appendix*, **ca**; *circa* = *about*, **cf** = *compare*, **esp** = *especially*, **et seq** = *and the following*, **f** = *and the following page*, **ff** = *and the following pages*, **ibid** = *in the same place*, **id**; **idem** = *by the same* (author), **inf** = *below*, **loc cit** = *in the place cited*, **ms** = *manuscript*; plural **mss**, **NB** = *take note of*, **nd** = *no date*, **op cit** = *in the work cited*, **passim** = *throughout*, **pl** = *plate*, **pp** = *pages*, **pub** = *published*, **qv** = *which see*, **ser** = *series*, **sup** = *above*, **suppl** = *supplement*, **trans** = *translated; translator*, **vide** = *see*, **viz** = *namely*.

hyd	hydraulic; hydrate.
hypo	sodium thiosulphate, formerly sodium hyposulphite.
Hz	hertz, unit of frequency.

I

I	Imperial; institute; island; Italy.
IATA	International Air Transport Association.
IBA	Independent Broadcasting Authority (formerly the **ITA** = Independent Television Authority).
ibid	**ibidem** = in the same place (*also* **ib**).
IBM	International Business Machines.
IBS	irritable bowel syndrome.
IC	Imperial College of Science and Technology, London (*also* **ICS**); identity card.
ic	integrated circuit; internal combustion.
2i/c	second in command.
ICA	Institute of Chartered Accountants; Institute of Contemporary Arts.
ICAN	International Commission for Air Navigation.
ICBM	Intercontinental Ballistic Missile (*also* **IBM**).
ICC	Imperial Cricket Conference; International Chamber of Commerce; International Correspondence Colleges.

ICCF	International Corresponding Chess Federation.
ICE	Institute of Chartered/Chemical/ Civil Engineers; International Cultural Exchange.
ICEF	International Council for Educational Films.
I Chem E	Institute of Chemical Engineers.
ICI	Imperial Chemical Industries.
ICIANZ	Imperial Chemical Industries, Australia and New Zealand.

I = The International Community

Just about every activity known to man has been elevated to international status, and the **I** for *International* abbreviation has proliferated on a truly global scale. Witness the **ICBD** (*International Council of Ballroom Dancing*); the **ICCAT** (*International Commission for the Conservation of Atlantic Tunas*); the **IFM** (*International Falcon Movement*) and this real whopper, the **IFCTUSETMSCT**, which stands for *International Federation of Christian Trade Unions of Salaried Employees, Technicians, Managerial Staff and Commercial Travellers*! International listings alone would fill a book this size so only the most important are listed here.

ICN	International Council of Nurses.
ICOM	International Council of Museums.
ICPO	International Criminal Police Organisation, *also* known as **Interpol**.

ICS	Imperial College of Science and Technology, London; International Correspondence School.
ICSU	International Council of Scientific Unions.
ICU	intensive care unit.
ICY	International Co-operation Year (1965).
ID	identification (card); Institute of Directors.
IDA	International Development Association; Industrial Diamond Association.
IDB	illicit diamond buyer.
IDL	international date line.
ie	*id est* meaning that is.
IEA	Institute of Economic Affairs; Institution of Engineers, Australia.
IFC	International Finance Corporation.
IFJ	International Federation of Journalists.
IFLA	International Federation of Library Associations.
IFTA	International Federation of Travel Agencies; International Federation of Teachers' Associations.
IGF	International Gymnastic Federation.
IGWF	International Garment Workers' Federation.
IGY	International Geophysical Year (1957–8).
IHF	International Hockey Federation.
IHRB	International Hockey Rules Board.
II	Roman numeral for two (2).
III	Roman numeral for three (3).
III	Investment in Industry Organisation.

ILC	International Law Commission.
ILEA	Inner London Education Authority.
ILGA	Institute of Local Government Administration.
ILGWU	International Ladies' Garment Workers Union.
ill	illustration; illustrator.
ILO	International Labour Organisation.
ILR	independent local radio.
IMF	International Monetary Fund; International Motorcycle Federation.
imp	impression (printing); imperial; imported.
IMPACT	implementation planning and control technique.
imperf	imperforate (philately).
in	inch (in^2 = square inch; in^3 = cubic inch).
IN	Indian Navy.
Inc	Incorporated.
inc	income.
INCB	International Narcotics Control Board.
incl	include; inclusive; incline.
ind	index; industrial; independent.
indef	indefinite.
inf	information (*also* **info**); infantry; inferior.
infra dig	*infra dignitatem* = undignified.
Inst	institute.
inst	instant; instrument.
INTELSAT	International Telecommunications Satellite Organisation.
Interpol	International Criminal Police Organisation.
inv	*invenit* = designed; *inv et del* = designed and drawn by (on prints and engravings).

IO	intelligence officer.
IOC	International Olympic Committee.
IOF	Independent Order of Foresters (Friendly Society).
I of M	Isle of Man (*also* **IoM, IOM**).
IOJ	International Organisation of Journalists.
IOOF	Independent Order of Oddfellows (lodge).
IoW	Isle of Wight; inspector of works (*also* **IW**).
IPA	Institute of Practitioners in Advertising; International Publishers' Association; India pale ale.
IPAA	International Prisoners' Aid Association.
IPARS	International Programmed Airline Reservation System.
IPC	International Publishing Corporation.
IPR	Institute of Public Relations.
ips	inches per second.
IPTPA	International Professional Tennis Players' Association.
IPU	Inter-Parliamentary Union.
IQ	intelligence quotient.
IR	Inland Revenue.
ir	inside radius.
IRA	Irish Republican Army.
iran	inspect and repair as necessary.
IRBM	intermediate-range ballistic missile.
IRC	International Red Cross.
IRF	International Rowing Federation.
IRO	International Refugee/Relief Organisation; Inland Revenue Office; industrial relations officer.
irreg	irregular.
IRS	Internal Revenue Service (US).

is	Island (*also* **I**).
ISC	Imperial Staff College; International Supreme Council (Freemasons).
ISD	International subscriber dialling.
ISF	International Shipping Federation.
ISIS	Independent Schools Information Service.
ISO	International Standards Organisation; Imperial Service Order.
ISPA	International Society for the Protection of Animals.
ISS	Institute for Strategic Studies.

Initials

Abbreviations are contractions, and therefore include initials, which are contractions of names: **GBS** for *George Bernard Shaw*, for example, or **NYC** for *New York City*. Other types of contractions are those of words, where all the middle letters are omitted (**Mr** for *Mister*); where the final letters are dropped (**cat** for *catalogue*); or where various bits of the word are dispensed with (**bldg** for *building*). An acronym results from the creative use of initials to coincide with a word, like **CAUTION** (*Citizens Against Unnecessary Tax Increases and Other Nonsense*) or to coin a new one, like **SNAFU** (*Situation Normal, All Fouled Up*).

| **ISSN** | International Standard Serial Number. |
| **ISU** | International Seamen's Union; International Skating Union. |

ITA	Independent Television Authority (now the IBA); Institute of Travel Agents/Air Transport.
ital	italic; italics.
Ital	Italy, Italian.
ITALY	I trust and love you.
IT & T	International Telephone and Telegraph Corporation.
ITC	Imperial Tobacco Company.
ITCA	Independent Television Contractors' Association.
ITGWF	International Textile and Garment Workers' Federation.
ITMA	catchphrase of 1940s radio comedian Tommy Handley, 'It's that man again!'
ITN	Independent Television News.
ITO	International Trade Organisation.
ITTF	International Table Tennis Federation.
ITU	International Telecommunications Union; International Temperance Union.
ITV	Independent Television.
ITWF	International Transport Workers' Federation.
iu	international unit.
IUD	intra-uterine device (*also* **IUCD**: intra-uterine contraceptive device).
IUS	International Union of Students.
IV	Roman numeral for four (4).
IVBF	International Volley-Ball Federation.
IWTA	Inland Water Transport Association.
IYHF	International Youth Hostels Federation.
IYRU	International Yacht Racing Union.

J

J	joule, unit of electric energy.
J & B	brand of Scotch whisky.
Jag	Jaguar car.
JAL	Japan Air Lines.
jan	janitor.
Jan	January (*also* **Ja**).
JAP	J. A. Prestwich & Co, motorcycle and other engines.
Jap	Japanese.
JATO	jet-assisted take-off.
JC	Jesus Christ; Jockey Club; Juvenile Court; Junior Chamber of Commerce (*also* **JAYCEE**).
JCB	Joseph Cyril Bamford, inventor of the internationally-used earth moving machines.
jct	junction.

Jes Coll	Jesus College, Oxford.
JETRO	Japan External Trade Organisation.
JFK	John Fitzgerald Kennedy, former US President; New York Airport.
JHS	junior high school.
JICNARS	Joint Industry Committee for National Readership Surveys.
jnr	junior (*also* **jr**).
joc	jocular.
jour	journal; journalist.
JP	Justice of the Peace.
jur	juror.
JRC	Junior Red Cross.
jt	joint.
Jul	July.
Jun	June.
jurisp	jurisprudence.
juv	juvenile.
JW	Jehovah's Witness (religious organisation).
JWB	Jewish Welfare Board.
jwlr	jeweller.
JWT	J. Walter Thompson (advertising agency).

K

K, k	Kelvin, or one kilowatt-hour; king; kopek; 1,000.
k & b	kitchen and bathroom.
KBC	King's Bench Court.
KBD	King's Bench Division.
KBE	Knight Commander of the Order of the British Empire.

kc	kilocycle.
KC	King's Counsel; Knight Commander; Kennel Club; Kansas City.
KCB	Knight Commander of the Most Honourable Order of the Bath.
KCMG	Knight Commander of the Most Distinguished Order of St Michael and St George.
KCVO	Knight Commander of the Royal Victorian Order.
Ken	Kensington, London (**S Ken** = South Kensington).
kg	kilogram (*also* **kilo**).
KG	Knight of the Most Noble Order of the Garter.
KGB	*Komitet Gosudarstvennoye Bezopasnosti* = Russian State Security Police.
KGC	Knight of the Grand Cross.
KGCB	Knight of the Grand Cross of the Bath.
KhZ	kilohertz (*also* **khz**).
kilo	kilogram (*also* **kg**; **kilog**).
KISS	Keep It Simple, Stupid.
KKK	Klu Klux Klan, US anti-black organisation.
KL	Kuala Lumpur, Malaysia.
KLM	*Koninklijke Luchtvaart Maatschappij* = Royal Dutch Air Lines.
km	kilometre (**km/h** = kilometres per hour).
kn	krona, Swedish unit of currency; krone, Danish and Norwegian currency unit.
KO	knock-out (boxing); kick-off.
K of C	Knight of Columbus (*also* **KC**).
kop	kopek, Russian unit of currency.

kpr	Keeper (**wkt kpr** = wicket keeper in cricket).
Kt	Knight; Karat (*See* **Ct** = carat).

Kt-KB$_3$, B-KN$_5$,

A thrilling chess game can be described in a couple of square inches of space, using internationally understood cryptic letters and numbers. To read chess moves you need to know the following abbreviations:

K	King	**Q**	Queen	**B**	Bishop
Kt	Knight	**R**	Rook	**P**	Pawn
–	moves to	**x**	takes	**Ch**	Check!
ep	*en passant*	**O-O**	Castles (**K**)	**O-O-O**	Castles (**Q**)
...	move made by black	**!**	good move	**?**	error

L

L	learner; Latin; Liberal (Party); *Linnaeus* (in botany); *Libra* = pound (£) sterling.
l	latitude; length; light; late; large; lease/leasehold; litre; lira (Italian currency unit).
LA	Los Angeles; Legislative Assembly.
Lab	Labour (Party); Labour Party supporter; Labrador.

lab	laboratory; labourer; label.
lag	lagoon.
lam	laminate.
LAM	London Academy of Music.
LAMDA	London Academy of Music and Dramatic Art.
Lancs	Lancashire.
LASER	light amplification by stimulated emission of radiation.
lat	latitude.
Lat	Latin (*also* **L**); Latvia.
LATCC	London air traffic control centre.
lav	lavatory.
lb	pound weight – avoirdupois.
LB	Bachelor of Letters.
LBC	London Broadcasting Company.
LBCH	London Bankers' Clearing House.
LBJ	Lyndon Baines Johnson, former US President.
LBS	London Graduate School of Business Studies.
lbw	leg before wicket (in cricket).
LC	Library of Congress (US); Lieutenant Commander.
L/C	letter of credit.
lc	lower-case (in typography); little change.
LCC	Former London Country Council (then **GLC**, abolished in 1986).
LCD	liquid crystal display; lowest common denominator.
LCM	London College of Music.
LD	Doctor of Letters.
ldg	landing; leading.
ldmk	landmark.
Ldn	London (*also* **Lon**).
LDP	Liberal-Democratic Party.
ldr	leader; ledger.
LE	Labour Exchange.

LEA	Local Education Authority.
LEB	London Electricity Board.
leg	legal; legation; legion; legislature; legitimate.
Leics	Leicester; Leicestershire.
LEPRA	Leprosy Relief Association.
LFB	London Fire Brigade.
LGB	Local Government Board.
lge	large; league.
lgth	length.
lh	left hand (**lhs** = left hand side.).
LI	Long Island (US); Lincoln's Inn, London.
lib	librarian; library; libretto.
Lib Cong	Library of Congress, Washington DC.
lic	licensed; licence.
Lieut	Lieutenant.
LIFO	last in first out.
LIHG	*Ligne Internationale de Hockey sur Glace* (International Ice Hockey Federation).
LILO	last in last out.
lim	limit; limited.
limo	limousine.
lin	linear; lineal; line.
Lincs	Lincolnshire.
lino	linoleum.
Lintas	Lever's international advertising service.
liq	liquid; liquor.
lit	literally; literature; literary.
litho	lithograph; lithography.
LittB	Bachelor of Letters/Literature.
LittD	Doctor of Letters/Literature.
LL	London Library.
lm	lumen (unit of light).
LMD	local medical doctor.
LME	London Metal Exchange.

Weights and measures

From Mr Owen Curtis

Sir, Talking to a nine-year-old about a packet of cheese I asked what "0lb 13¼oz" meant. She did not know what lb and oz signified.

With all the care and thought that goes into the science of packaging maybe lb and oz should be replaced by the words pounds and ounces.

Best wishes,
OWEN CURTIS,
53 Victoria Avenue,
Hull, Humberside.
February 25.

This letter to *The Times* (2/3/92) demonstrates how the meaning of even commonplace abbreviations can go missing.

LMH	Lady Margaret Hall, Oxford.
LMR	London Midland Region of British Rail.
LMS	London, Midland and Scottish Railway (formerly).
L Mus	Licentiate in Music.
LNER	London and North Eastern Railway (formerly).
Lnrk	Lanarkshire.
LNWR	London and North Western Railway (formerly) (*also* **L & NWR**).
LOA	leave of absence.
loc	location; local; letter of credit.
Lond	London.
LOX	liquid oxygen.
LP	long playing record; Labor Party; life policy.
LPE	London Press Exchange.

LPN	Licensed Practical Nurse.
LPO	London Philharmonic Orchestra; local post office.
LPS	London Philharmonic Society.
LRCA	London Retail Credit Association.

LRCVS et al

A person with letters after his or her name beginning with **L** is likely to be a Licentiate – the holder of a certificate of competence from a professional organisation, in this case a *Licentiate of the Royal College of Veterinary Surgeons*. Others you are likely to meet with are **LRIBA** (*Licentiate of the Royal Institute of British Architects*) and **LRCM** (*Licentiate of the Royal Academy of Music*).

Lrs	Lancers.
LRT	London Regional transport.
LS	Linnean Society; Licentiate in Surgery; Law Society; long shot (in film-making); licensed surveyor.
ls	signed letter (**als** = autograph signed letter).
LSD	The hallucinogenic drug lysergic acid diethylamide; pounds, shillings and pence (**£sd**); League of Safe Drivers.
LSE	London School of Economics; London Stock Exchange.
LS & GCM	Long Service and Good Conduct Medal.
LSO	London Symphony Orchestra.

LST	local standard time.
Lt	Lieutenant.
LTA	Lawn Tennis Association.
LTAA	Lawn Tennis Association of Australia.
LTB	London Transport/Tourist Board.
Lt Col	Lieutenant-Colonel.
Ltd	Limited (company).
ltr	letter; litre.
lub	lubricate; lubricant.
lug	luggage
LV	luncheon voucher; licensed victualler.
lv	low voltage.
LVA	Licensed Victuallers' Association.
lw	long wave (frequency).
LW	low water.
lwb	long wheel base.
LWL	load waterline.
LWM	low water mark.
LWONT	low water, ordinary neap tide.
LWOST	low water, ordinary spring tide.
LWT	London Weekend Television.

M

M	*Monsieur* (French); mark (German currency); Monday.
m	male; masculine; married; metre; medium; memorandum; mile; *mille* (French for 1000); million; maiden over (in cricket, an over in which the batsman fails to score).

MA	Master of Arts; *Missionarius Apostolicus* (Apostlic missionary).
MA & F	Ministry of Agriculture and Fishing.
mac	Macintosh (style of raincoat).
mach	machinery.
MAD	mutual assured destruction; mean absolute deviation.
MADD	Mothers Against Drunken Driving (US).
mag	magazine; magnetic; magnitude.
Magd	Magdalen College, Oxford.
MAN	*Maschinenfabrik Augsburg-Nurnberg AG* (Germany).
Man Dir	Managing Director (*also* **MD**).
m & b	mild and bitter (ale).
M & Ms	button-size chocolate-coated sweets.
M & S	Marks and Spencer, department stores.
Man Ed	Managing Editor.
MANWEB	Merseyside and North Wales Electricity Board.
mar	married; marine; maritime.
Mar	march.
marg	margarine.
mart	market.
mas	masculine (*also* **masc**).
MASH	Mobile Army Surgical Hospital (US).
mat	matrix; matte; matinee; maternity; mature.
maths	mathematics.
Matric	Matriculation (entry examination).
max	maximum.
MAYDAY	Help Me (from the French *m'aidez*) distress call.
MB	medical board; marketing board; methyl bromide (fire retardant).

mb	millibar.
MBA	Master of Business Administration.
mbr	member.
mc	motorcycle (*also* **m/c**); megacycle.
MC	Master of Ceremonies; Military Cross; Member of Congress (US); Master of Surgery.
MCC	Marylebone Cricket Club; Melbourne Cricket Club.
MCP	male chauvinist pig.
MCPS	Mechanical Copyright Protection Society; Member of the College of Physicians and Surgeons.

Inapt Acronyms

The American philologist William Safire tells an amusing story against himself when, during the Presidential campaign of 1972 he was asked to check the name of the Committee to Re-elect the President. He ran through a range of acronymous possibilities – **CTRTP**, **Comrep**, **CrePres**, and so on, and gave the name a clean bill of health. Unfortunately he missed one; the Committee later became famous as **CREEP**. At about the same time, an equally inapt acronym popped up for the Law of the Sea Treaty, forever after known as **LOST**.

MCU	medium close-up (cinematography).
MD	Managing Director; Doctor of Medicine; mentally deficient; Musical Director.
MDA	Muscular Dystrophy Association.
Mddx	Middlesex.
mdr	minimum daily requirement.

ME	Middle East; mechanical/mining engineer; myalgic encephalomyelitis.
med	medical; medicine; median; medium; medieval.
MEF	Mediterranean Expeditionary Force.
MEK	methyl ethyl ketone, an industrial solvent.
Melb	Melbourne.
mem	member; memorial.
Mencap	Royal Society for Mentally Handicapped Children and Adults.
MEP	Member of the European Parliament.

Masters and Members

Once again, there are hundreds of initials of professional credentials beginning with **M**. Here are a few you might come across:

MIAA	Member Architect of the Incorporated Association of Architects and Surveyors.
MIBE	Member of the Institution of British Engineers.
MIMechE	Member of the Institution of Mechanical Engineers.
MIMT	Member of the Institute of the Motor Trade.
MIRTE	Member of the Institute of Road Transport Engineers.
MInstT	Member of the Institute of Technology.
MS(Dent)	Master of Surgery (Dental Surgery).

Mer	Merionethshire.
Merc	Mercedes (car).
MERLIN	Medium Energy Reactor, Light Water Industrial Neutron Source.
Messrs	*Messieurs* (French) = gentlemen.
Met	Metropolitan Opera House, New York.
met	meteorological; metropolitan.
metall	metallurgical.
Meth	Methodist.
meths	methylated spirits.
Metro	*Chemin de fer métropolitan* (Paris underground).
MFB	Metropolitan Fire Brigade.
MFD	minimum fatal dose.
MFH	Master of Fox Hounds.
mfr	manufacture; manufacturer (**mfd** = manufactured).
MG	Morris Garage sports car.
mg	milligram; morning.
MGM	Metro-Goldwyn-Mayer, Hollywood film studios.
MGN	Mirror Group Newspapers, the media company formerly owned by the late Robert Maxwell.
mgt	management.
MHA	Methodist Homes for the Aged.
MHF	medium high frequency.
MHR	Member of the House of Representatives.
MHW	mean high water.
MHWNT	mean high water, neap tide.
MHWST	mean high water, spring tide.
MHz	megahertz.
MIA	missing in action.
MICR	magnetic-ink character recognition.
MIDAS	missile defence alarm system.
MIF	milk in first (before pouring tea, considered non-U).

MIG, MiG	Russian fighter aircraft, designed by MIkoyan and Gurevich.
Mil	Military.
mill	*millionen* (German million).
MIMS	Monthly Index of Medical Specialties.
min	minimum; mineralogy; minute; minor.
MIRV	Multiple Independently Targeted Re-entry Vehicle.
misc	miscellaneous.
Miss	Mistress, formerly a woman of easy virtue, now a modern, respectable unmarried woman.
MIT	Massachusetts Institute of Technology.
MITI	Ministry of International Trade and Industry (Japan).
MJQ	Modern Jazz Quartet.
mk	mark; mark (German currency); (**mkd** = marked).
mkt	market.
MLC	Member of the Legislative Council.
MLD	minimum lethal dose.
Mlle	*Mademoiselle* (French = Miss).
MLR	minimum lending rate.
MLS	medium long shot (in cinematography).
MLWNT	mean low water, neap tide.
MLWST	mean low water, spring tide.
mm	millimetre (**mm**^{2} = square millimetre; **mm**^{3} = cubic millimetre).
MM	Military Medal; Mercantile Marine.
Mme	*Madame* (French = Mrs).
Mmes	*Mesdames* (French = Ladies).
MMQ	minimum manufacturing quantity.
mng	Managing (ie, Mgn Dir = Managing Director).

mngr	manager (*also* **mgr**); **mngmt** = management.
mo	month; also used to indicate the size of a book's page, as in **12mo**, **24mo**, **32mo** and **64mo**, where a sheet is folded and cut to form 12, 24, 32 and 64 pages respectively.
Mo	Monday.
MO	money order; Medical Officer; Meteorological Office.
MOD	Ministry of Overseas Development; Ministry of Defence.
MODEM	Modulator/Demodulator (computer term).
Moho	Mohorovicic Discontinuity: the boundary between the earth's crust and mantle, named after its discoverer, the Croatian geologist Andrija Mohorovicic (1857–1930).
MOMA	Museum of Modern Art, New York City.
Mon	Monmouthshire (*also* **Monm**); Monday.
M1	M One, Treasury estimate of money in circulation.
M1, M2, B2065 etc.	Designation for British roads. Those prefixed with an M are motorways; the A prefix indicates a Class 1 road; the B prefix indicates a Class 2 road.
Mons	*Monsieur* (*also* **M**), French = Mr.
Moped	Motorised pedal cycle.
MOPS	Mail Order Protection Scheme.
MOR	middle of the road (radio music).
MORI	Market and Opinion Research International.
MOT	Motor Vehicle Test Certificate.
Mounty	Royal Canadian Mounted Police.

MOUSE	Miniature Orbital Unmanned Satellite, Earth.
MP	Member of Parliament; Military Police; Mercator's projection (in cartography).
MPA	Music Publishers' Association.
mpc	maximum permissible concentration.
mpg	miles per gallon.
mph	miles per hour.
MPO	Military Post Office.
MPTA	Municipal Passenger Transport Association.
Mr	Mister; Master.
MR	map reference; Master of the Rolls.
MRH	Member of the Royal Household.
Mrs	Missus (prefix for a married woman).
MRT	Mass Rapid Transport.
Ms	prefix for women, married or unmarried (pronounced Mizzz or Muzzz or something in-between).
MS	multiple sclerosis; medium shot (in film-making).
m/s	metres per second.
MSA	Malaysian Singapore Airways.
MSc	Master of Science.
msc	miscellaneous.
MSG	monosodium glutamate, a food flavour enhancer.
Msgr	Monsignor (RC Church).
mt	mount; mountain.
MTB	motor torpedo boat.
M3	Treasury estimate of total money supply, including money deposited in banks and institutions.
MU	Musicians' Union; Manchester United Football Club.
mum	mother; chrysanthemum.

mun	municipal.
MV	motor vessel; market value.
MVO	Member of the Royal Victorian Order; male voice over (on TV and film scripts).
MVS	Master of Veterinary Science (*also* **MVSc**).
MW	Master of Wine.
mW	milliwatt.
MY	motor yacht.
MYOB	mind your own business.
myth	mythological; mythology.

MI5, MI6 and the Secret World

MI5 is the branch of the British Intelligence organisation responsible for internal security and counter-espionage in Britain. **MI6** is the branch responsible for international espionage. The US has its **FBI** and **MI–8,** and the Republic of Ireland its **G2.** Spies love abbreviations! Then, in Britain, there is **MI1** (Directorate of Military Intelligence); **MI3** (the former German Section, Military Intelligence); **MI8** (the Radio Security Service); **MI11** (Field Security Police) and **MI9** (Escape and Evasion Service). Not surprisingly, each of these clandestine outfits spawns even more shadowy initials: **D1** (Head of Russian counter-esponiage, now presumably out of job); **SF** (Phone tapping service); **GC & CS** (Government Code and Cipher School); **IIC** (Industrial Intelligence Centre) and the Butlins of the spy world, **WX** (Camp WX, Isle of Man).

N

N	north; northern; Norway; National; London postal district.
n	name, near, negative; nephew; noon; north; northern; noun; number; neutral; normal.
n/a	not available.
NAACP	National Association for the Advancement of Coloured People.
NAAFI	Navy, Army and Air Force Institutes (*also* **Naffy**).
NAB	National Assistance Board; National Association of Broadcasters.
NAC	National Advisory/Anglers'/Archives Council.
NACF	National Art Collections Fund.
nad	no appreciable difference; nothing abnormal detected.
NAfr	North Africa.
NAGS	National Allotments and Gardens Society.
NAHA	National Association of Health Authorities.
NALGO	National and Local Government Officers' Association.
NAMH	National Association for Mental Health.
NAPF	National Association of Pension Funds.
NAPO	National Association of Property Owners.
nar	narrow.
NAS	Noise Abatement Society; National Association of Schoolmasters.

NASA	National Aeronautics and Space Administration (US).
nat	natural; national; nationalist; native.
NATCS	National Air Traffic Control Service.
NATE	National Association for the Teaching of English.
NATO	North Atlantic Treaty Organisation.
NATSOPA	National Society of Operative Printers and Assistants (former printing union).
NATTKE	National Association of Theatrical, Television and Kine Employees (former entertainment trade union).
NatWest	National Westminster Bank.
nav	naval; navigable; navigation (*also* **navig**).
Nazi	*Nationalsozialisten*, former National Socialist Party member (Germany).
nb	*nota bene* = note well; no ball (in cricket).
NBA	Net Book Agreement; National Boxing/Basketball Association (US).
NBC	National Broadcasting Company (US).
nbg	no bloody good.
nc	no charge (*also* **n/c**).
NCA	National Cricket Association.
NCB	National Coal Board; no claim bonus.
NCC	Nature Conservancy Council (Britain).
NCCL	National Council for Civil Liberties.

NCCVD	National Council for Combating Venereal Diseases.
NCR	National Cash Register Company; no carbon required.
NCU	National Cyclists' Union.
nd	no date (ie, undated); no decision; not drawn.
NDA	National Dairymens' Association.
Ndl	The Netherlands.
NDP	Net Domestic Product.
née	née (French = born) ie, Mrs Joan Smith, née Jones indicates that Mrs Smith's maiden name was Jones.
NEA	North East Airlines.
NEB	National Enterprise Board; *New English Bible*.
NEC	Nippon Electrical Company (Japan).
ne'er	never.
neg	negative.
Neg	Negro.
NESB	non-english speaking background (applied to some foreign immigrants in Australia).
NESTOR	NEutron Source Thermal reactOR.
net	after all deductions (*also* **nett**).
Neth	Netherlands.
neur	neurological.
neut	neutral.
N/f	no funds (*also* **nf**).
NF	National Front.
NFA	National Federation of Anglers.
NFL	National Football League (US).
NFS	not for sale.
NFT	National Film Theatre, London.
NFU	National Farmers' Union.
NFUW	National Farmers' Union of Wales.

NFWI	National Federation of Womens' Institutes.
NFYFC	National Federation of Young Farmers' Clubs.
ng	no good; narrow gauge (railway).
NGA	National Graphical Association.
NGS	National Geographic Society.
NHI	National Health Insurance.
NHK	*Nippon Hoso Kyokai* (Japan Broadcasting Corporation).
NHS	National Health Service.
NI	National Insurance; Northern Ireland; News International.
Nimby	not in my backyard.
N Ire	Northern Ireland (*also* **N Ir**).
NIREX	Nuclear Industry Radioactive waste disposal EXecutive.
NJ	nose job.
NKr	Norwegian krone (currency unit).
NKVD	*Narodny Komissariat Vnutrennikh Del* (Russian People's Commission of Internal Affairs).
NLF	National Liberation Front, Vietnam (*also* in Yemen).
nlt	not later than; not less than (**nmt** = not more than).
NMGC	National Marriage Guidance Council.
NMHA	National Mental Health Association.
NMU	National Maritime Union.
no	number; north; northern.
No 10	10 Downing Street, London (Prime Minister's residence); No 1 London = Apsley House, Piccadilly, former home of the Duke of Wellington.
nom	nomenclature; nominated; nominal.

non res	non-resident.
non-U	unacceptably unfashionable.
nos	numbers.
NOP	National Opinion Poll.
Nor	Norway.
nor	normal; northern.
Northants	Northamptonshire.
Northmb	Northumberland.
NORWEB	North Western Electricity Board.
NORWICH	(k)Nickers Off Ready When I Come Home.

An Initial Quiz

The answer to each of these questions is a single initial or letter from the first half of the alphabet. *Answers on page 81.*

1 Second most famous early Ford car (not the T Model)?
2 Scrabble tile with a value shared by no other letter?
3 First letter on the standard Snellen eye test chart?
4 Highest key on an ordinary piano?
5 A learner-driver of a car must display it?

Notts	Nottinghamshire.
Nov	November.
NoW	*News of the World*, Sunday newspaper.
np	new pence, introduced with decimalisation; new paragraph (printing); nickel plated.
n/p	net proceeds (*also* **np**).

NPA	National Pigeon Association; Newspaper Publishers' Association.
NPFA	National Playing Fields Association.
nr	near.
NRA	National Rifle Association, Bisley.
NRC	Nuclear Research Council.
NRCA	National Retail Credit Association.
NRF	National Relief Fund.
NRFL	Northern Rugby Football League.
NRS	National Readership Survey.
NSA	National Skating Association.
NSC	National Safety Council.
nsf	not sufficient funds (*also* **n/s**).
NSFGB	National Ski Federation of Great Britain.
NSMAPMAWOL	*Not So Much a Programme, More a Way of Life* (former BBC TV programme).
NSPCC	National Society for the Prevention of Cruelty to Children.
NSW	New South Wales, Australia.
NT	National Theatre, London; National Trust; Northern Territory (Australia); New Testament.
NTSC	National Television System Committee (regarding standards for US colour television).
NTV	Nippon Television.
NUJ	National Union of Journalists.
num	numerical.
NUM	National Union of Mineworkers.
NUPE	National Union of Public Employees.
NUR	National Union of Railwaymen.
NURA	National Union of Ratepayers' Associations.
NUS	National Union of Students/Seamen.

Answers to Initial Quiz

1 The Ford Model A
2 The letter K
3 The letter F
4 High C
5 L for Learner

NW	North-western; North Wales; north-west London postal district.
NWAWWASBE	Never wash a window with a soft boiled egg (a slogan from the 40s radio show ITMA).
NYC	New York City.
NYD	not yet diagnosed.
NYO	National Youth Orchestra.
NYPD	New York Police Department.
NYSE	New York Stock Exchange.
NYT	National Youth Theatre.
NZ	New Zealand.

O

O	human blood type.
o	owner; only; over (in cricket).
O & E	Operations and Engineering.
O & M	Ogilvie & Mather, advertising agency.
OAP	old age pensioner.
OAS	*Organisation de l'armée secrète* (former pro-French political organisation in Algeria).

OB	outside broadcast; Old Bailey; old bonded whisky.
OBAFGKMRNS	The Draper classification of stars according to temperature and brightness (mnemonic: *Oh Be A Fine Girl, Kiss Me Right Now, Susan*).
OBE	Order of the British Empire.
obit	obituary.
obj	object; objective.
obs	obsolete (*also* **obsol**); obscure; observer; obstetrician; obstetrics.
Obs	the *Observer* Sunday newspaper.
oc	ocean; office copy; over the counter.
o'c	o'clock.
occ	occupation; occasional; occurrence.
OCR	optical character recognition/ reader.
Oct	October.
oct	octavo (printing).
OCUC	Oxford and Cambridge Universities' Club.
OD	overdose (**OD**'d = overdosed).
O/D	overdrawn; overdraft; on demand.
ODESSA	Ocean Data Environmental Sciences Services Acquisition.
ODETTE	Organisation for Data Exchange Through Tele-Transmission in Europe.
ODP	overall development planning.
OECD	Organisation for Economic Co-operation and Development.
OEDIPUS	Oxford English Dictionary Interpretation, Proofing and Updating System.
o'er	over.
off	official (*also* **offic**); office; officer.

OFT	Office of Fair Trading.
OFTEL	Office of Telecommunications.
og	own goal (in football).
OGM	ordinary general meeting.
OGPU	Russian state political administrative department, forerunner of the **KGB**.
oh	overhead (*also* **o/h**); on hand.
ohc	overhead camshaft.
OHD	organic heart disease.
OHMS	On Her Majesty's Service.
OHN	occupational health nurse.
ohv	overhead valve.
OIT	Organisation international du travail (International Labour Organisation).
ojt	on the job training.
ok	all right; everything in order.
Okie	American midwest migrant workers during 1930s.
OLC	Oak Leaf Cluster (military award).
Old Test	Old Testament.
O-level	Ordinary level examinations for the General Certificate of Education.
OM	Order of Merit; ordnance map.
OMM	*Officier de l'Ordre du Mérite Militaire*, French military decoration.
on appro	on approval.
ono	or near offer.
Ont	Ontario, Canada.
ont	ordinary neap tide.
OOD	officer of the deck.
OOG	officer of the guard.
ooo	of obscure origin (dictionary term).
o/o/o	out of order.
007	British Secret Service codename for Ian Fleming's fictional character James Bond.

OOW	officer of the watch.
op	operation; operator; operational; opposite (*also* **opp**); optical; opaque.
OP	out of print; old people.
Op art	optically influenced designs, launched in the 1960s.
OPC	ordinary Portland cement.
OPEC	Organisation of Petroleum Exporting Countries.
OPEX	operational, executive and administrative personnel.
ophth	opthalmic.

OP and OAPs

The search is on for a more dignified term than old age pensioner (**OAP**), with its frail, toothless, threadbare image. Senior Citizen is perhaps an improvement, and other ideas are under consideration like **WOTCHA** (*wonderful Old Thing Considering Her/His Age*); **TEPID** (*Tastes Expensive, Pension Inadequate, Dammit!*) and **HOPEFUL** (*Hard-up Old Person Expecting Full Useful Life*).

---

opp	opposite (*also* **op**); opposed.
opr	Operator.
OR	official receiver; orderly room; other ranks.
or	overhaul and repair (*also* **o/r**).
ORBIS	orbiting radio beacon ionospheric satellite.
ORBIT	on-line retrieval of bibliographical information.

orch	orchestra.
ord	ordained; ordinary; ordnance.
org	organisation; organic; organ.
orn	ornithology; ornamental.
orth	orthopaedic; orthography.
o/s	out of stock (*also* **OS**); out of service; outsize.
OS	Ordnance Survey.
o'seas	overseas.
OSS	Office of Strategic Services (US).

OZ Abbrs

Australians are loth to use long words and they are ferocious verbal surgeons. But they also have the curious habit of adding an 'o' at the end of abbreviated words:

arvo	afternoon	**garbo**	garbage collector
aspro	aspirin	**kero**	kerosene
commo	communist	**metho**	methylated spirit
doco	documentary	**preggo**	pregnant

---

osteo	osteopathic; osteopath.
OT	overtime; occupational therapy; Old Testament (*also* **Old Test**).
OTB	off-track betting (US).
otc	over the counter.
OTC	Officer Training Corps.
OU	Oxford University.
OUP	Oxford University Press.
ov	over; overture.
OWLS	Oxford Word and Language Service.
Oxon	*Oxonia* = Oxford; Oxford University

Oxbridge	Oxford-Cambridge; also used to describe the older, classical universities in the UK.
OXFAM	Oxford Committee for Famine Relief.

P

P	park; parking; Post Office (on maps); postage; pawn (in chess); pedestrian; Protestant; public; positive; port.
p	page; paragraph; passed (in exams); peso, peseta and piastre (currencies); pint; population; present.
PA	personal assistant; Patients' Association; personal allowance (taxation); public address (system); press attaché; prosecuting attorney; Publishers' Association.
P/A	power of attorney; private account.
PAA	Pan American Airways (*also* **PanAm**).
PABX	Private Automatic Branch eXchange (telephone system).
PAC	Pacific Air Command (US).
Pac	Pacific.
PACE	Precision Analogue Computing Equipment; performance and cost evaluation.
pad	paddock.
PAL	Phase Alternation Line (British TV standard).

Pal	palaeontology; palace; Palestine.
Pan	Panama.
pan	panachromatic (photography).
Pan-Am	Pan-American Airways.
P & G	Procter & Gamble (manufacturers).
p & p	postage and packing.
panto	pantomime.
Pap-NG	Papua-New Guinea.
par	paragraph; parallel; parish; parochial.
paras	parachute troops.
Parl	Parliament; parliamentary.
pass	passenger; passenger train.
PATA	Pacific Area Travel Association.
Pat	patent (**Patd** = patented; **Pat pend** = patent pending).
PAWC	Pan-African Workers' Congress.

POMS, POMMIES and POMEs

As usual, the British and the Australians will argue forever about the derivation of **Pommie**, the nickname by which Englishmen are known Down Under. A reddish or sunburned complexion, likened to an apple, or, worse, a pomegranate? Well, no. The most accepted etymology is a term supposedly used during the early nineteenth-century convict era when most immigrants in Australia were unwilling *Prisoners of Mother England* or **POMEs**, later shortened to **POMS**.

PAX	Private Automatic telephone eXchange.

PAYE	Pay As You Earn (income tax payment system).
pbi	poor bloody infantry.
PBM	Permanent benchmark (in surveying).
PBX	Private Branch telephone eXchange.
PC	Police Constable (*also* **Pc**); Privy Councillor; parish council.
pc	per cent; percentage; postcard; personal computer.
PCC	Parochial church council.
pcl	parcel.
PCZ	Panama Canal Zone.
pd	paid; passed; postage due; post dated (*also* **p/d**).
PD	Police Department; production department.
pdq	pretty damn quick.
PE	Physical Education; probable error.
P/E	price–earnings ratio; port of embarkation.
Pem	Pembrokeshire (*also* **Pemb**).
PEN Club	Poets, playwrights, Editors, essayists and Novelists.
PEPS	personal equity plan(s) (savings).
per	on behalf of (shortened from *per procurationem*); period; person.
per an	per annum = for the year.
per cent	by the hundredths (ie, six per cent or 6% = six hundredths of the whole).
perf	perforated (philately); performance.
perk	perquisite (*usually* **perks**).
perm	permanent wave (hairstyle); permutation.
perp	perpendicular.
pers	personal; person.

pet	petroleum; petrology.
Pf	pfennig (German currency unit).
Pfc	Private first-class (US Army).
pg	page.
PG	parental guidance required (motion picture classification).
PGA	Professional Golfers' Association.
pH	measurement scale of acidity and alkalinity.
ph	phase; philosophy (*also* **phil**); philosopher.
pharm	pharmacy; pharmacist; pharmacy (*also* **phar**).
Phil	Philadelphia, USA (*also* **Phila**; **Philly**); Philharmonic; philology; Philippines.
phon	phonetically; phonetic.
PHS	Printing House Square (former address of *The Times*).
phys	physician; physicist; physical.
physiol	physiological.
physog	physiognomy.
PI	per inquiry; petrol injected; programmed instruction.

PIX, NIX and Varietyese

The US show business journal *Variety* published one of the world's greatest abbreviated headlines: **HIX NIX PIX IN STIX**, meaning that country movie-goers were not fans of films about rural America. If you can translate a headline like this you will have no trouble with **HANK CINQ** (when Olivier's *Henry V* bombed in the US); nor with **HIP NIP IN HUB** (Japanese jazzman performing in Boston).

pic	picture (usually photographic); pictorial.
PIE	Paedophile Information Exchange.
PIN	Personal Identification Number.
PinC	Priest-in-Charge.
pix	motion pictures.
pk	park (*also* **P**); pack.
pkg	package.
pkt	packet.
pl	place; plain; plural.
PL	Plimsoll line (safe loading line on ships).
P & L	profit and loss.
PLA	Port of London Authority; People's Liberation Army (People's Republic of China).
PLATO	Programmed Logic for Automated Learning Operation.
plc	public limited company.
PLN	Nationalist party, Nicaragua.
PLO	Palestine Liberation Organisation.
PLP	Parliamentary Labour Party.
PLR	Public Lending Right (makes payments to authors on books loaned by public libraries in the UK).
plu	plural.
Plum	Pelham – nickname for two celebrities: the comic author Sir Pelham Grenville Wodehouse; and the English cricketer Sir Pelham Warner.
PLUTO	pipe line under the ocean (supplied Allied forces in Europe during World War II).
Ply	Plymouth.
PM	Prime Minister; Police Magistrate.
pm	*post meridiem* = after noon; post mortem; post master.

PMG	Postmaster General.
pmh	past medical history.
pmk	postmark.
PMS	pre-menstrual syndrome; Pantone Matching System (colour printing).
PMT	pre-menstrual tension; photo mechanical transfer (graphics).
pmt	payment.
PND	post-natal depression.
png	*persona non grata* = unacceptable person.
pntr	painter.
PO	Post Office; postal order; pilot officer; petty officer; personnel officer; power operated.
po	chamberpot.
P & O	Peninsular and Oriental Steam Navigation Company.
POB	Post Office box.
POC	port of call.
POD	pay on delivery.
Pol	Poland.
pol	police; polarise; political; politician.
Polio	poliomyelitis.
POLIS	Parliamentary On-Line Information Service.
Poly	polytechnic; polyvinyl; Polynesia.
pop	population; point of purchase; popular (music).
por	portion; porous; portrait (*also* **port**).
PORIS	Post Office Radio Interference Station.
porn	pornography.
Port	Portugal.
port	portrait; portable.
pos	point of sale; position; positive.
posn	position.

POSH

Professional etymologists have attacked the popular belief that the word POSH – meaning rich and classy – derives from 'port outward, starboard home', the desirable and cooler and thus more expensive cabins on ships travelling between England and India. The philological argument simmers on, but romance, apparently, is stronger than logic, and the popular belief remains undented.

POSSLQ	person of opposite sex sharing living quarters.
posthum	posthumous (*also* **post**).
POUNC	Post Office Users' National Council.
POV	point of view (in film-making); privately owned vehicle.
POW	prisoner of war.
PP	parliamentary papers; parish priest; past president.
pp	pages; *per procura* = by proxy; post paid; pre-paid; parcel post; privately printed.
PPA	Pools Proprietors' Association; Periodical Publishers' Association.
ppd	post-paid; prepaid.
PPL	private pilot's licence.
ppm	parts per million.
PPP	Penelope's Pony Paddock (term used by estate agents to describe a small field attached to a country cottage); private patient's plan; personal pension plan.

pps	*post post scriptum* = an additional postscript.
PPS	Parliamentary Private Secretary.
PQ	parliamentary question.
PR	public relations; proportional representation; Puerto Rico; postal regulations; progress report.
pr	pair; per; present; print; printer; painter; price.
pram	perambulator.
PRB	Pre-Raphaelite Brotherhood (nineteenth-century artists' group).
preb	prebendary.
pref	preface; preference; preferable; prefect.
prefab	pre-fabricated.
prelim	preliminary; **prelims** = introductory pages in a book.
premed	premedical (often preparations prior to operating).
prep	preparatory; preparation (school).
pres	present.
Pres	President; Presbyterian.
prev	previous; previously.
pri	private (*also* **pvt**; **priv**); priority.
Prin	Principal; Principality.
PRO	public relations officer; Public Record Office.
pro	professional.
pro-am	professional–amateur (in sport).
prob	probable; problem; probate.
proc	proceedings (eg. **Proc Roy Soc** = *Proceedings of the Royal Society*); process.
prod	producer; production; product.
Prof	Professor.
prog	programme; prognosis; progressive.

prole	proletarian.
prom	promenade (concert).
pron	pronounced.
prop	property (**props** = theatrical property); proposition; propeller; proprietor; proprietary; proper.
Prot	Protestant.
pro tem	*pro tempore* = for the time being.
prov	provincial; province; provisional; proverb.

Mind Your Ps and Qs

There are various derivations for this peculiar catchphrase, meaning, 'Look sharp, be careful and behave properly'. One has it that **'p's and 'q's** meant pints and quarts, probably of ale; the admonition warned either against over indulgence, or of being overcharged. Another explanation is that printers, in the days of setting type by hand, had to watch their 'p's and 'q's as they looked much the same.

Provo	Provisional member of the Irish Republican Army.
PRS	Performing Right Society Ltd.
Pru	Prudential Assurance company Ltd.
PS	public school; Philological Society.
ps	*post scriptum* = postscript.
PSA	pleasant Sunday afternoon.
PSAB	Public Schools Appointments Bureau.
PSB	Premium Savings Bond.
pseud	pseudonym; pseudo.

psi	pounds (lbs) per square inch, measure of pressure.
PSI	Policy Studies Institute.
PT	Public Trustee; pupil teacher.
pt	part; pint; point; past tense.
PTA	Parent-Teachers Association; Passenger Transport Authority.
PT boat	patrol torpedo boat.
ptd	painted; printed.
PTE	Passenger Transport Executive.
ptg	printing.
PTI	physical training instructor.
PTO	please turn over; power take-off.
pt/pt	point to point (horse racing).
PTS	Philatelic Traders' Society.
pub	public house; published; publisher (**pub date** = date on which a book is published).
pud	pudding; pick up and deliver.
pug	pugilist.
punc	punctuation.
pur	purchase; purchased; purple; purify.
PVA	polyvinyl acetate.
PVC	polyvinyl chloride.
PVR	premature voluntary retirement.
pvte	private (*also* **pvt**; **pte**).
PWA	Public Works Administration (US) (formerly).
PWD	Public Works Department.
PWR	pressurised water reactor.
PX	physical examination.
pxt	*pinxit* = he/she painted it (*also* **pinx**, **pnxt**).
PYO	pick your own.

Q

Q	Queen; coulomb (electrical unit); Queensland; quality; quartermaster; quetzal (Guatemala currency).
q	quarter; quarterly; quart; quarto; question; query; quire; quantity.
Q & A	question and answer.
qango	quasi-autonomous non-governmental organisation.
QANTAS	Queensland and Northern Territory Aerial Service, Australian airline.
QB	Queen's Bench (**QBD** = Queen's Bench Division).
Qbc	Quebec.
QC	Queen's Counsel; Queen's College.
QE2	Queen Elizabeth II, Cunard Line cruise ship.
QED	*quod erat demonstrandum* = which was to be proved.
QF	quality factor.
QGM	Queen's Gallantry Medal.
QHP	Queen's Honorary Physician.
QHS	Queen's Honorary Surgeon.
Qld	Queensland.
QMG	Quartermaster-General.
qnty	quantity (*also* **q, qty, qlty**).
QPM	Queen's Police Medal.
QPR	Queens Park Rangers Football Club.
qr	quarter; quarterly; quire.
QS	quarantine station.
quad	quadrangle; quadrant; quadruple.
quake	earthquake.

Some Curious Qs

If you can convince others that **Qantas** is a word and not an acronym, you might also convince them that it is the only Q-word or name where the Q is not followed by a U. But is it? There is qwerty and there are some spellings of Arabic names (Aqaba, Qataba, Qaf, Qom and Qaddafi) that dispense with the U, and in the 1960s there was a nylon fibre called Qiana. Then there is a character in James Bond novels called Q, which was also the *nom de plume* of the real-life author Sir Arthur Quiller-Couch. All without the U, but all proper names, unfortunately. QED (Quite Easily Done). But keep it on the QT (quiet = secret).

qual	qualification.
qualgo	quasi-autonomous non-governmental organisation.
quango	*see* **qango**, the alternative form.
qv	*quod vide* = which see.

R

R	registered (mail); railway; Réaumur (degree of heat); river; Republic; Republican; right; route; Registered at the US Patent Office.
r	radius; rare; right; red; road; rod; retired; rouble (Russian currency unit); runs (in cricket); rain.

RA	Royal Academy; Royal Academician; Ratepayers' Association; Referees' Association; Royal Artillery; Ramblers; Association.
R & A	Royal and Ancient Golf Club, St Andrews, Scotland.
RAA	Royal Academy of Arts.
RAAF	Royal Australian Air Force.
RAC	Royal Automobile/Aero Club; Royal Agricultural College, Cirencester.
RACE	rapid automatic checkout equipment.
RACON	radar beacon.
Rad	Radnorshire, Wales.
rad	radius; radian; radar; radio; radiology; radiation absorbed dose.
RADA	Royal Academy of Dramatic Art.
RADAR	Radio Detection And Ranging.
RADAS	Random Access Discrete Address System.
R Adm	Rear Admiral.
RAF	Royal Air Force.
RAH	Royal Albert Hall, London.
RAI	*Radio Audizioni Italiane* = Italian Broadcasting Corporation.
RAM	random access memory.
RAMAC	random access memory accounting.
RAN	Royal Australian Navy.
R & B	rhythm and blues (music).
R & CC	riot and civil commotions.
R & D	research and development.
r & r	rest and recreation; rock 'n' roll (music).
RBA	Royal Society of British Artists.
rbl	rouble, Russian currency unit.

RBS	Royal Society of British Sculptors.
RC	Roman Catholic; Red Cross; Reformed Church.
rc	reinforced concrete.
RCA	Royal College of Art; Radio Corporation of America.
RCAF	Royal Canadian Air Force.
RCMP	Royal Canadian Mounted Police.
RCN	Royal Canadian Navy.
RCSB	Royal Commonwealth Society for the Blind.
RCVS	Royal College of Veterinary Surgeons.
R/D	refer to drawer (unwelcome notation on cheque).
RDA	recommended daily allowance (medical and nutrition).
RDC	Rural District Council.
RDZ	radiation danger zone.
Re	rupee (currency unit of India, Pakistan and Ceylon) (also **Rs**).
rec	received; receipt; recent; record; recreation.
recce	reconnaissance.
recd	received (*also* **rec**).
rect	rectangular; rectify.
ref	referee; refer; reference; refund (*also* **refd**).
reg	registered; regular; regulation; regiment.
REGAL	range and elevation guidance for approach and landing.
regd	registered.
Reg prof	Regius Professor.
Reg TM	Registered Trade Mark (*also* **RTM**).
rej	reject.
rel	relative; religion; relic; release.
rem	remarks.

Renf	Renfrewshire, Scotland.
rep	representative; repeat; repertory (theatre); reprint; repaired; report.
repl	replace; replacement.
repo	repossess (ie, the **repo man** who comes to repossess).
repro	reproduction.
req	request; requisition; required.
res	residence; resident; reserved; reservoir; research; reservation; resolution.
resig	resignation.
rest	restaurant (*also* **restr**).
ret	return; returned.
retd	retired; returned; retained.
Rev	Reverend.
rev	reverse; revolutions; revised; revision; review; revenue.
rew	reward.
RF	Royal Fusiliers; rugby football.
RFL	Rugby Football League.
RFSU	Rugby Football Schools' Union.
RFU	Rugby Football Union.
rgd	registered.
RGS	Royal Geographical Society.
Rgt	Regiment (**rgtl** = regimental).
Rh	Rh Factor = Rhesus Factor, inherited agglutinating agent in blood, first observed in rhesus monkeys).
RH	Royal Highness; relative humidity.
rh	right hand.
RHA	Regional Health Authority.
rhd	right hand drive.
rheo	rheostat.
rhino	rhinoceros.
R Hist S	Royal Historical Society.
rhp	rated horsepower.
RHS	Royal Horticultural Society.

RI	Royal Institution, London; Royal Institute of Painters in Water Colours.
RIA	Royal Irish Academy.
RIAC	Royal Irish Automobile Club.
RIAI	Royal Institute of Architects in Ireland.
RIAM	Royal Irish Academy of Music.
RIBA	Royal Institute of British Architects.
RIC	Royal Irish Constabulary; Royal Institute of Chemistry.
RIIA	Royal Institute of International Affairs.
RIP	*requiescat in pace* = rest in peace.
RIS	Radio Interference Service.
RKO	Radio Corporation of America/Keith-Orpheum Theatres: from 1921–1953 one of the big Hollywood studios.
RL	Rugby League.
RLF	Royal Literary Fund.
RLPAS	Royal London Prisoners' Aid Society.
RLPO	Royal Liverpool Philharmonic Orchestra.
RLS	Robert Louis Stevenson, Scottish writer and poet.
RLSS	Royal Life Saving Society.
rly	railway (*also* **rlwy**); relay.
RM	Royal Marines; registered midwife; Royal Mail.
rm	room (**rms** = rooms).
RMC	Royal Military College.
R Months	The eight months with 'r' in their names during which it is claimed oysters may safely be eaten.
RN	Royal Navy.
RNC	Royal Naval College.

RNIB	Royal National Institute for the Blind.
RNID	Royal National Institute for the Deaf.
RNVR	Royal Naval Volunteer Reserve.
RNZAF	Royal New Zealand Air Force.
RNZN	Royal New Zealand Navy.
ro	run out (in cricket); rowed over (in rowing).
ROAM	return on assets managed.
ROI	return on investment; Royal Institute of Oil Painters.
Rolls	Rolls-Royce (*also* **Roller**) cars and engines.
ROM	read-only memory.
rop	run of paper (in newspaper publishing).
RORC	Royal Ocean Racing Club.
RORO	roll on–roll off car and truck ferry.
RoSPA	Royal Society for the Prevention of Accidents.
rot	rotary.
ROW	right of way.
Roy	Royal; royalty.
RP	Royal Society of Portrait Painters; reply paid.
Rp	rupiah, Indonesian currency unit.
rph	revolutions per hour.
RPI	retail price index.
rpm	revolutions per minute; reliability performance measure.
RPO	Royal Philharmonic Orchestra; railway post office.
rpt	repeat; reprint; report.
RR	railroad (US); Rolls-Royce.
RRB	Race Relations Board.
RRP	recommended retail price.
RS	Royal Society.
RSA	Royal Scottish Academy/Academician.

RSC	Royal Shakespeare Company.
RSE	Royal Society of Edinburgh.
RSI	Royal Sanitary Institute.
RSI	Repetitive Strain Injury.
RSJ	rolled steel joist.
RSL	Returned Services League (of Australia); Royal Society of Literature.
RSM	regimental sergeant major; Royal Society of Medicine; Royal School of Mines; Royal Society of Musicians.
RSNC	Royal Society for Nature Conservation.
RSNZ	Royal Society of New Zealand.
RSPB	Royal Society for the Protection of Birds.
RSPCA	Royal Society for the Prevention of Cruelty to Animals.
RSSPCC	Royal Scottish Society for the Prevention of Cruelty to Children.
RSVP	*Répondez s'il vous plait* = please reply.
RSWS	Royal Scottish Water Colour Society.
rt	right.
RTA	road traffic accident.
RTB	return to base.

The Three Rs

These are readin', 'ritin' and 'rithmetic. The phrase supposedly originated during the early years of the nineteenth century, when during a banquet Sir William Curtis, an illiterate Lord Mayor of London, proposed a toast to education.

rtd	returned; retired (**rtd ht** = retired hurt in cricket).
RTDS	real time data system.
RTE	*Radio Telefís Éireann* (Irish radio and television).
rte	route.
rtg	rating.
Rt Hon	Right Honourable.
RTM	Registered trade mark.
rtn	return; retain.
Rt Rev	Right Reverend.
rtw	ready to wear.
RTZ	Rio Tinto Zinc Corporation.
RU	Readers' Union; Rugby Union.
RUA	Royal Ulster Academy of Painting, Sculpture and Architecture.
RUC	Royal Ulster Constabulary.
rugger	rugby football.
RUI	Royal University of Ireland.
RUPP	road used as public path.
RUR	Karel Capek's 1921 play about Rossum's Universal Robots.
Rus	Russia (*also* **Russ**).
RV	Revised Version (of the Bible); rateable value.
RVCI	Royal Veterinary College of Ireland.
RVO	Royal Victorian Order.
RYA	Royal Yachting Association.
RYS	Royal Yacht Squadron.

S

S	south; southern; summer; Sunday; Saint; socialist; *Señor; Signor; Signora*.

s	south; southern; small; shilling; single; slow.
SA	South Africa; South Australia; *Société Anonyme* (French/Belgium limited liability company); *Sociedad Anónima* (Spanish limited company); Saudi Arabia; subject to approval.
SAA	South African Airways.
SAAA	Scottish Amateur Athletic Association.
SAAB	*Svensk Aeroplan Aktiebolag* (Swedish aircraft and car manufacturer).
SAAF	South African Air Force.
Sab	Sabbath.
SABA	Scottish Amateur Boxing Association.
SABC	South African Broadcasting Corporation.
SABENA	*Société anonyme belge d'exploitation de la navigation aérienne*, Belgian airline.
SABRA	South African Bureau of Racial Affairs.
SAC	Scientific Advisory Council; Scottish Automobile Club.
SADF	South African Defence Force.
SADIE	Scanning Analogue to Digital Input Equipment.
SAE	Society of British Automotive Engineers; stamped addressed envelope.
SAFE	South African Friends of England.
SAG	Screen Actors' Guild (US).
SAID	Sexual Allegations in Divorce.
Salop	Shropshire.
SALT	Strategic Arms Limitation Talks (US and former USSR).

SAM	surface-to-air missile.
san	sanitary; sanitorium.
s & m	sadism and masochism, commonly sadomasochism, or the fantasy of causing and receiving pain; sausages and mash.
SANE	Schizophrenia A National Emergency.
SANDS	Stillborn And Neonatal Death Society.
SANR	subject to approval, no risk.
SANROC	South African Non-Racial Olympics Committee.
sans	*sans* = without (eg, sans serif is a style of typeface without serifs or lines at the end of the letters).
SAR	search and rescue.
SAS	Scandinavian Airlines System.
SAT	scholastic aptitude test (USA).
Sat	Saturday; satellite; Saturn.
SATCO	signal automatic air traffic control system.
sax	saxophone.
SAYE	save as you earn.
sb	single-breasted (suit style).
SBA	School of Business Administration.
SBH	Scottish Board of Health.
SC	School Certificate; Senior Counsel; Supreme Court
Sc	science; sculptor; Scandinavia; Scotland.
sc	scale; sculptor; *sculpsit* = carved or engraved; self contained; small capitals (typesetting); single column.
Scan	Scandinavia (*also* **Sc**; **Scand**).
s caps	small capitals (typesetting).
SCARAB	Submerged Craft Assisting Repair And Burial.

SCB	Speedway Control Board.
scc	single column centimetre (print advertising).
SCE	Scottish Certificate of Education.
SCGB	Ski Club of Great Britain.
sch	school; scholar; scholarship; schedule.

An Abbreviated Quiz

Here are some abbreviations for various measurements. See if you can match the measurement with the item being measured. *Answers on page 109.*

1	22kt	**A**	light bulb
2	70dB	**B**	car engine
3	20 in diag	**C**	gold ring
4	2B	**D**	can of soft drink
5	12 fl oz	**E**	noise
6	100w	**F**	television set
7	4000 rpm	**G**	load of coal
8	5 cwt	**H**	pencil

Sch	schilling, Austrian currency unit.
sched	schedule (*also* **sch**).
sci	single column inch (print advertising).
sci-fi	science fiction.
SCOFF	Society for the Conquest Of Flight Fear.
SCOOP	Stop Crapping On Our Property (warning to dog owners).
Scot	Scotland; Scottish; Scotsman.
SCPS	Society of Civil and Public Servants.

scr	script; scruple.
Script	Scriptural; Scripture.
scuba	Self Contained Underwater Breathing Apparatus.
sculp	sculptor; sculpture.
SCUM	Society for Cutting Up Men (a creation of feminist Valeria Solanis who shot and wounded artist Andy Warhol in 1968).
SDA	Scottish Development Agency; Seventh Day Adventist.
SDO	senior duty officer.
SDP	Social Democratic Party.
SDS	scientific data system.
SE	Stock Exchange (*also* **S/E**; **S/Ex**).
SEACOM	telephone cable system connecting Asian mainland to Australia and New Guinea.
SEATO	South East Asia Treaty Organisation.
SEC	Securities and Exchange Commission (US).
sec	secretary (*also* **secy**); second; sector.
SECAM	*sequential couleur à mémoire*, French-developed television broadcasting system.
SED	Scottish Education Department.
SEEA	*Société européenne d'énergie atomique* = European Atomic Energy Society.
Seeboard	South-Eastern Electricity Board.
seg	segment.
sel	select; selected; selection.
semi	semi-detached house.
Sen	Senator; Senate.
sen	senior (*also* **sr**; **senr**).
Sen M	Senior Master.
Sen Mist	Senior Mistress.

Sept	September.
ser	series; serial; sermon.
SERPS	State Earnings-Related Pension Scheme.
ser	service; servant.
sew	sewer; sewerage.
SF	San Francisco; science fiction; Sinn Fein.
SFA	Scottish Football Association; Sweet Fanny Adams = absolutely nothing.
SFI	*Société Financière Internationale* = French International Finance Corporation.

Abbreviated Quiz Answers

1–C; 2–E; 3–F; 4–H; 5–D; 6–A; 7–B; 8–G

SFL	Sequenced Flashing Lights (airport approach); Scottish Football League.
sg	specific gravity (*also* **sp gr**).
sgd	signed.
sgl	single.
sh	second-hand (*also* **s/h**); shilling; share (*also* **shr**); sheep; sheet.
SHA	Scottish Hockey Association.
Shak	Shakespeare (*also* **Sh**; **Shake**).
shd	should.
shouse	euphemistic abbreviation for shithouse.
SI	Most Exalted Order of the Star of India; Staten Island, New York State; seriously ill.
SIA	Society of Investment Analysts.

SIB	Savings and Investment Bank; Securities and Investment Board.
sic	thus written, as in the original.
sig	signature; signal.
sing	singular.
SIS	Secret Intelligence Service.
SISTER	Special Institutions for Scientific and Technological Education and Research.
sit	situation.
sit rm	sitting room.
SITA	Students' International Travel Association.
sitcom	situation comedy (type of television programme).
SI unit	*Système International unit* = International System of Units.
SIW	self-inflicted wound (*also* **SIM** = self-inflicted mutilation).
SJ	Society of Jesus (Jesuits).
SJAA	St John Ambulance Association.
SJAB	St John Ambulance Brigade.
SKC	Scottish Kennel Club.
S Ken	South Kensington, London.
SKF	*Svenska Kullagerfabriken* = Swedish Ball Bearing Company, large steelmaking organisation.
S Kr	Swedish krona, currency unit.
SL	sea level.
SLADE	Society of Lithographic Artists, Designers, Engravers and Process Workers.
Slav	Slavonic.
SLC	Scottish Leaving Certificate.
sld	sold; sealed, sailed.
S Ldr	Squadron Leader.
SLP	Scottish Labour Party; Socialist Labour Party.
SLR	single lens reflex (camera).

SLTA	Scottish Licensed Trade Association.
SLV	standard (*or* space) launch vehicle.
SM	sales manager; stage manager; station master; silver medallist.
sm	small.
SMATV	satellite master antenna television.

SMERSH

SMERSH was not an Ian Fleming invention for his James Bond spy novels, but a real department of Russian intelligence which had the motto, *smert shpionen*, or 'death to spies'. Its most famous victim was Lev Trotsky.

SMJ	Sisters of Mary and Joseph.
SMO	Senior Medical Officer.
SMS	secondary modern school.
SMTA	Scottish Motor Trade Association.
SN	serial number; service number.
s/n	signal to noise ratio.
SNAFU	situation normal, all fouled up.
SNCF	*Société nationale des chemins de fer français* = French national railways.
snd	sound.
SNFU	Scottish National Farmers' Union.
SNO	Scottish National Orchestra.
SNOBOL	string-oriented symbolic language (computers).
SNP	Scottish National Party.
snr	senior (*also* **sr**).
Sñr	*Señor* = Mr; *also* **Sr** (Spanish).
Snra	*Senhora* = Mrs (Portuguese).

Sñra	*Señora* = Mrs; *also* **Sra** (Spanish).
Snrta	*Senhorita* = Miss (Portuguese).
Sñrta	*Señorita* = Miss (Spanish).
SO	Scottish Office; standing order; seller's option.
SOB	silly old bugger; son of a bitch (US).
soc	socialist; society; slightly off colour.
Soc Dem	Social Democrat.
sociol	sociology; sociologist.
SOCONY	Standard Oil Corporation of New York.
SODOMEI	Japanese Federation of Trade Unions.
SOE	Special Operations Executive.
SOGAT	Society Of Graphical and Allied Trades.
SOHIO	Standard Oil Company of Ohio.
sol	soluble; solution.
SOL	shit on the liver (US).
solv	solvent.
sonar	sound navigation and ranging.
SOP	standard operating procedure.
sop	soprano.
SOR	sale or return.

SOS

It is commonly believed that the distress call **SOS** is an acronym for 'Save Our Souls'; or 'Save Our Ship'. In fact, it stands for three call letters of the Morse Code (. . . – – – . . .) or three dots, three dashes, three dots) which were judged to be the easiest and clearest to be sent by someone in distress.

Sou	south; southern; Southampton.
Sov	Soviet.
sov	shut off valve; sovereign.
SP	starting price (race betting); stop payment.
Sp	Spain; Spanish; spring.
sp	single phase (electrical); special; species; speed; sport; special position (newspaper advertising).
Spam	spiced ham, a proprietary brand of canned pork.
SPC	Society for the Prevention of Crime.
SPCK	Society for Promoting Christian Knowledge.
spec	specification; special; specimen; speculation.
specs	spectacles; specifications.
SPECTRE	SPecial Executive for Counter-inTelligence, Revenge and Extortion, the fanciful terrorist organisation in Ian Fleming's James Bond novels.
SPG	Society for the Propagation of the Gospel.
sp gr	specific gravity (*also* **sg**).
SPNC	Society for the Promotion of Nature Conservation.
SPOT	sattelite positioning and tracking.
SPQR	*Senatus Populusque Romanus* = the Senate and people of Rome; small profits, quick return.
SPRINT	solid-propellant rocket-intercept missile.
sprl	*société de personnes à responsabilité limitée* = a French private limited company.
Spurs	Tottenham Hotspur Football Club.
SPVD	Society for the Prevention of Venereal Disease.

Squd Ldr	Squadron Leader (*also* **S Ldr**).
sq in	square inches (*also* **sq ft** = square foot; **sq yd** = square yard; **sq m** = square metre, etc.).
SR	Southern Railway (formerly); sodium ricinoleate (in toothpaste).
sr	senior (*also* **snr**); self-raising (flour).
SRO	sold right out; standing room only.
SRS	*Societatis Regiae Sodalis* = Fellow of the Royal Society.
SRU	Scottish Rugby Union.
SS	*Schutzstaffel* = former Nazi 'blackshirts', Hitler's elite personal army; Sunday school; social security; secret service; Secretary of State; steamship.
ss	stainless steel.
s/s	same size.
SSAFA	Soldiers' Sailors' and Airmens' Families Association.
SSFA	Scottish Schools' Football Association.
S/Sgt	Staff Sergeant.
SSHA	Scottish Special Housing Association.
SSPCA	Scottish Society for the Prevention of Cruelty to Animals.
SSSI	site of special scientific interest.
SST	supersonic transport.
SSTA	Scottish Secondary Teachers' Association.
ST	*The Sunday Times*; spring tide.
St	Saint (**Ste** = *Sainte* = female saint).
st	street; state; stone (14 lbs weight); stanza; stumped (in cricket).
1st	first.
stab	stabiliser; stabilised.
Staffs	Staffordshire.

stand	standard (*also* **std**); standardised.
St And	St Andrews, Scotland.
stat	statistic (**stats** = statistics); stationary.
Stat Hall	Stationers' Hall, London.
stbd	starboard.
STC	Satellite Test Centre (US); state total cost; Samuel Taylor Coleridge, English poet; Sydney Turf Club.
STD	subscriber trunk dialling; sexually transmitted disease.
std	standard.
sten	stenographer.
ster	stereotype; £ sterling.
stg	£ sterling (*also* **ster**).
STGWU	Scottish Transport and General Workers' Union.
Sth	south; southern (*also* **sthn**).
Stipe	Stipendiary Magistrate (*also* **Stip**).
stk	stock.
STL	studio-to-transmitter link.
stn	station.
STO	standing order; senior technical officer.
STOL	short take-off and landing (aircraft).
STOP	Students Tired Of Pollution.
STOPP	Society of Teachers Opposed to Physical Punishment.
stp	standard temperature and pressure.
str	straight; strength; strong; structural.
STR	surplus to requirements (**STIR** = surplus to immediate requirements).
Strad	Stradivarius violin.
strep	streptococcus.
stud	student.

STV	subscription television; standard test vehicle; Scottish Television Limited.
Su	Sunday; Sudan.
sub	subject; subscription; submarine; subsidiary; substitute; suburb; sub-editor.
subd	subdivision.
subj	subject (*also* **sub**).
Sub L	Sub-Lieutenant (*also* **Sub Lt**; **Sub-Lieut**).
Suff	Suffolk.
suff	sufficient.
Sult	Sultan; sultana.
sum	summary.
Sun	Sunday.
SUNFED	Special United Nations Fund for Economic Development.
sup	superior; superfine.
supp	supplement; supplementary (*also* **suppl**).
supr	supervisor (*also* **Supvr**).
Supt	Superintendent.
sur	surface; surplus.
Sur	Surrey.
surv	survey; surveyor.
SUS	Students' Union Society; Scottish Union of Students.
SV	safety valve.
s/v	surrender value (insurance).
svg	saving (**svgs** = savings).
svp	*s'il vous plait* = if you please.
SW	south-west; South Wales; Senior Warden; small woman.
sw	sea water; short wave.
SWA	South West Africa.
SWACS	space warning and control system.
SWALK	sealed with a loving kiss.
SWAPO	South West Africa People's Organisation.

swb	short wheel base.
swbd	switchboard.
SWET	Society of West End Theatre Managers.
SWF	single white female.
SWIE	South Wales Institute of Engineers.
SWIMS	Study of Women in Men's Society (US).
SWL	safe working load (on cranes and derricks).
SWMF	South Wales Miners' Federation.
SWOT	Strengths, Weaknesses, Opportunities, Threats: formula used in marketing analysis of new products.
SWP	safe working pressure.
Sx	Sussex.
Syd	Sydney, New South Wales.
S Yd	Scotland Yard.
syl	syllabus (*also* **syll**).
sym	symptom; symbol; symbolic; symmetrical.
symph	symphony.
syn	synonym; synchronise; synthetic.
syr	syrup.
syst	System; systematic.

T

T	telephone (on maps).
t	teaspoonful; taken; time; tense; ton weight; town; temperature.
TA	telegraphic address; Territorial Army; table of allowances.
T/A	temporary assistant; technical assistant.

TAA	Trans-Australia Airlines.
tab	table; tabulate; tablet.
TAB	standard typhoid vaccine.
tach	tachometer.
Tai	Taiwan.
TAL	traffic and accident loss.
Tal	*Talmud Torah*, Jewish laws and traditions.
TAM	Television Audience Measurement; tactical air missile.
tan	tangent.
T & A	Tits'n'Ass, used to describe certain magazines and tabloid news-papers.
t & b	top and bottom.
T & CPA	Town and Country Planning Association (*also* **TCPA**).
t & e	test and evaluation.
t & g	tongue and groove (timber).
T & O	taken and offered (in betting).
T & SG	Television and Screen Writers' Guild.
TAP	*Transportes Aéreos Portugueses* = Portuguese Airlines.
tarmac	bituminous surfacing, after tar + John McAdam, pioneering roadmaker.
Tas	Tasmania.
TASS	*Telegrafnoje Agentsvo Soviet-skovo Sojuza* = Russian telegraphic press agency.
TAT	transatlantic telephone cable.
Tatts	Tattersall's, Australian lottery company.
TB	tuberculosis; Treasury Bill.
tb	true bearing (navigation).
tba	to be announced; tyres, batteries and accessories.
tbcf	to be called for.

tbd	to be decided.
TBM	temporary benchmark; tactical ballistic missile.
tbs	tablespoon; tablespoonful (*also* **tbsp**).
TC	town clerk; training centre; Trinity College.
tc	traveller's cheque; temperature control; twin carburettors; terra cotta; true course (navigation).
TCB	Thames Conservancy Board.
TCCB	Test and County Cricket Board.
tchr	teacher (**tchg** = teaching).
TCM	Trinity College of Music, London (*also* **TCL**).
TCP	*trichlorophenylmethyliodialicyl* = antiseptic.
TD	Teaching Diploma
tdc	top dead centre (engineering).
te	twin-engined (*also* **t/e**); trailing edge; turbine engine; thermal efficiency.
TEA	Terminal Education Age – age at which individuals leave school, college or university.
tec	detective.
tech	technical; technician.
TEFL	Teaching English as a Foreign Language.
teg	top edges gilt (book binding).
tel	telephone; telegram; telegraphic (*also* **tele**, **teleg**).
telex	teletype exchange message.
telly	television.
tel no	telephone number.
temp	temperature; temporary.
ten	tenant.
ter	terrace (*also* **terr**).
terr	territory; territorial; terrace.

term	terminal; terminate; terminology.
tert	tertiary.
TES	*The Times Educational Supplement.*
Tesco	T. E. Stockwell and Sir John Cohen, key supplier and founder of the grocery chain store respectively.
Tessa	Tax Exempt Special Savings Account.
test	testimony.
TFA	total fatty acids.
tfr	transfer.
TGIF	thank God it's Friday.
tgt	target.
TGV	*train à grand vitesse* = French high speed passenger train.
TGWU	Transport and General Workers' Union.
TH	Trinity House (**THWM** = Trinity high water mark; **TLWM** = Trinity low water mark).
Thai	Thailand.
theol	theology; theological.
theor	theoretical; theorem.
therm	thermometer.
THES	*The Times Higher Education Supplement.*
Thur	Thursday (*also* **Th**).
TI	Texas Instruments Corporation (US); Tourist Information Bureau (*also* **TIB**).
TIR	*transport international des marchandises par la route* = European twenty-six-country agreement allowing road trucks to bypass frontier customs until reaching their final destination.
TIS	technical information service.
tit	title; titular.

TKO	technical knockout (in boxing).
tks	thanks (*also* **thnks**).
tkt	ticket.
TLC	tender loving care.
TLs	typed letter, signed.
TLS	*The Times Literary Supplement*.

Jokey Abbreviations

Most people know what **SNAFU** means, but how about **SUSFU** (*Situation Unchanged; Still Fouled Up*) and **REPULSE** (Russian Efforts to Publish Unsavoury Love Secrets of Edgar)? The latter acronym refers to the former FBI chief J. Edgar Hoover; its purpose was, you might say, **OTE** on Hoover's death (*OverTaken by Events*). On the other hand, it might have been subject to **FUBB** (*Fouled Up Beyond Belief*).

TM	trademark; transcendental meditation; Their Majesties; technical memorandum.
tm	true mean (navigation).
tmbr	timber.
TML	three mile limit (shipping).
TN	true north.
TNT	trinitrotoluene, high explosive.
TO	take-off; turn over (*also* **t/o**); telegraphic order; transport/technical officer.
tob	tobacco.
Toc H	Christian help organisation founded in 1915 by the Rev 'Tubby' Clayton. Toc = Army signal for the letter T, for Talbot House, the movement's headquarters.

TOD	time of delivery; The Open Door, an organisation that helps phobia sufferers.
Tok	Tokyo.
TOMCAT	Theatre of Operations Missile Continuous-wave Anti-tank Weapon.
tonn	tonnage.
topog	topographical; topography.
Tor	Toronto, Canada.
TOS	temporarily out of stock/service.
Toshiba	Tokyo Shibaura Electrics, Japanese electronics company.
tot	total.
tote	totalisator.
tour	tourist; tourism.
tourn	tournament.
TP, tp	to pay; town planner; taxpayer; test panel; true position.
TPI	Tax and Price Index.
TPO	Tree Preservation Order.
TPR	temperature, pulse and respiration.
tpt	trumpet; transport (*also* **transp**).
TR	Territorial Reserve; tracking radar; test run.
tr	track; train; transfer; truck; treasurer; trustee; trainee; transpose; translate; transport.
trad	traditional.
trannie	transistor radio, usually portable.
trans	transaction; translation; transpose; transport.
transl	translation; translate.
Trd	Trinidad.
Tre	Treasurer (Government).
Treas	Treasury.
trf	tariff; tuned radio frequency.
trg	training.
trig	trigonometric.

Trip	Tripos, final examination for Cambridge University honours degree.
TRO	temporary restraining order.
trop	tropical.
trs	transfer; transpose.
TRSB	time reference scanning beam.
TS, ts	training ship; typescript; till sale; temperature switch; tensile strength; test summary.
TSB	Trustee Savings Bank.
tsp	teaspoonful; teaspoon.
TSS	Toxic Shock Syndrome.
TT	Tourist Trophy (eg, Isle of Man **TT** Motorcycle races); telegraphic transfer; teetotaller; tuberculin tested (dairying); transit time.
TTA	Travel Trade Association.
TTFN	Ta-ta for now, catchphrase of radio comedian Tommy Handley.
TTTC	Technical Teachers Training College.
TU	trade union; thermal unit.
Tu	Tuesday (*also* **Tue**, **Tues**).
TU–144	Tupolev supersonic aircraft, one in a series named after designer Andrei Tupolev.
TUC	Trades Union Congress.
TUCC	Transport Users' Consultative Committee.
TUCGC	Trades Union Congress General Council.
turb	turbine; turboprop.
turps	turpentine.
TV	television; test vehicle; terminal velocity.
TVA	Tennesee Valley Authority (US); *taxe à la valeur ajoutée* = French value added tax.

TVP	textured vegetable protein.
tw	tail wind.
TWA	Trans-World Airlines.
TWO	this week only.
TWOC	taking without owner's consent (police term for car theft) (*also* **TAWOC**: take away without owner's consent).
TW3	*That Was The Week That Was* (1960s BBC programme).
TWU	Transport Workers' Union.
TYC	Thames Yacht Club.
TYO	two-year-old.
typo	typographical error.
typog	typography; typographer.
typw	typewritten.

U

U	Universal Certificate for motion pictures (may be seen by unaccompanied children); Burmese equivalent of Mr (eg, former Burmese Prime Ministers U Nu and U Ne Win); University; urinal.
UA	United Artists Corporation; under age.
UAA	United Arab Airlines.
UAE	United Arab Emirates.
u & lc	upper and lower-case (lettering and typography).
UAOD	United Ancient Order of Druids (Friendly Society).

UIAA et al

There are scores of abbreviations beginning with the letters **UI**. In almost all cases these are international unions of like organisations abbreviated from the French title: **UIAA** is the *Union internationale des associations d'announceurs*, which is the International Union of Advertisers' Associations. You are unlikely to need intimate acquaintance of many of them, including the **UIEIS** (*International Union for the Study of Social Insects*) and the **UIMP** (*International Union for Protecting Public Morality*). But, then, who knows?

UAP	United Australia Party.
UAU	Universities Athletic Union.
U-Boat	*Unterseeboot* = submarine (German).
UBR	University Boat Race (between Cambridge and Oxford).
UBS	United Bible Societies.
UC	University College; urban council.
UCC	Univeral Copyright Convention.
UCCA	Universities Central Council on Admissions.
UCD	University College, Dublin.
UCH	University College Hospital, London.
UCHD	usual childhood diseases (*also* **UCD**).
UCI	*Union cycliste internationale* = International Cyclists' Union.
UCL	University College, London; upper cylinder lubricant.
UCLA	University of California at Los Angeles.

UCTA	United Commercial Travellers' Association of Great Britain and Ireland.
UCW	University College of Wales.
UDA	Ulster Defence Association.
UDC	Urban District Council.
UDF	Ulster Defence Force.
UDI	Unilateral Declaration of Independence.
UDR	Ulster Defence Regiment.
UEA	University of East Anglia.
UEFFA	Union of European Football Associations.
UER	university entrance requirements; *Union européenne de radio-diffusion* = European Broadcasting Union; unsatisfactory equipment report.
UF	United Free Church of Scotland.
UFO	unidentified flying object.
uhf	ultra high frequency.
uht	ultra high heat (treatment).
uhv	ultra high voltage.
U/I	under instruction.
UK	United Kingdom, which includes Britain (England, Wales and Scotland) and Northern Ireland (Channel Islands and Isle of Man are not part of the UK, but Crown dependencies within the British Isles).
uke	ukulele.
Ukr	Ukraine.
ulf	ultra low frequency.
ULICS	University of London Institute of Computer Science.
ULP	University of London Press.
ult	ultimate, ultimately.
UMFC	United Methodist Free Churches.
un	united; unified; union.

UN

United Nations – an organisation that, like the EEC after it, has begat a vast family of programmes, committees, commissions, administrations and agencies. Of at least 100 or so, here are a few that are worth knowing:

UNCIO	United Nations Conference on International Organisation.
UNEC	United Nations Education Conference.
UNECA	United Nations Economic Commission for Asia.
UNEDA	United Nations Economic Development Administration.
UNEF	United Nations Emergency Force.
UNESCO	United Nations Educational, Scientific and Cultural Organisation.
UNFAO	United Nations Food and Agriculture Organisation.
UNGA	United Nations General Assembly.
UNICEF	United Nations Children's Fund.
UNIDO	United Nations Industrial Development Organisation.
UNIO	United Nations Information Organisation.
UNISCAT	United Nations Expert Committee on the Application of Science and Technology.
UNO	United Nations Organisation.
UNREF	United Nations Refugee Emergency Fund.
UNRRA	United Nations Relief and Rehabilitation Administration.
UNRWA	United Nations Relief and Works Agency for Palestinian Refugees.
UNSG	United Nations Secretary General.
UNSR	United Nations Space Registry.
UNWCC	United Nations War Crimes Commission.

unauth	unauthorised.
uncir	uncirculated.
UNCLE	United Network Command for Law Enforcement (from the TV programme, *The Man from UNCLE*).
uncond	unconditional.
uncor	uncorrected.
undergrad	undergraduate.
undtkr	undertaker.
unexpl	unexplored; unexplained; unexploded.
univ	university (*also* **uni**); universal.
UNIVAC	universal automatic computer.
unm	unmarried.
unsat	unsatisfactory.
UP	United Press; United Presbyterian; Uttar Pradesh (India); Ulster Parliament.
up	underproof (alcohol).
upd	unpaid.
uphol	upholstery.
UPI	United Press International.
UPS	United Parcel Service (US).
UPU	Universal Postal Union.
ur	urine; urinary.
urb	urban.
URC	United Reformed Church.
Urd	Urdu.
urg	urgent.
URT	upper respiratory tract infection.
Uru	Uruguay.
US	United States; unsaleable.
USA	United States of America.
USAF	United States Air Force.
USDA	United States Department of Agriculture.
USG	United States Government; United States gallon.

USLTA	United States Lawn Tennis Association.
USMC	United States Marine Corps.
USNR	United States Naval Reserve.
USO	United Service Organisation, a recreation and entertainment facility for US forces.
USP	unique selling proposition.
US Pat	United States registered patent.
USS	United States ship.
USVI	United States Virgin Islands.
usw	ultra short wave.
UTA	Ulster Transport Authority.
ute	utility = pick-up truck (Australia).
Utd	United.
UTDA	Ulster Tourist Development Association.
UU	Ulster Unionist.
U-V	ultra-violet (*also* **uv**, **UV**; **UVL** = ultra-violet light).
uw	underwater; unladen weight.
UXB	unexploded bomb.

V

V, v	see **The Versatile 'V'**, p. 130.
V1, V2	*Vergeltungswaffe* = German rocket-launched bombs used against Britain during World War II.
VA	Royal Order of Victoria and Albert; Veterans' Adminstration (US).
VAC	Vector analogue computer.
vac	vacancy; vacant; vacuum.
vacc	vaccination.

VAD	Voluntary Aid Detachment (to the Red Cross).
vag	vagrant.
val	valuation; valuable.
van	advantage (in tennis).
V & A	Victoria and Albert Museum, London.
v & t	vodka and tonic.
var	variety; variable; variation.
VARIG	*Empresa de Viacão Aérea Rio Grandense*, major Brazilian airline.

The Versatile 'V'

The letter V is probably the most commonly used initial, and is also of some antiquity; it still represents the Roman numeral 5. But it also stands for (in lower case): very, volume, village, valley, vicarage, vicar, volt, voltage, valve, ventilator, vowel, verb, verso, vice (as in v pres), vertical, vein, versus, visibility, velocity, victory, and no doubt many more meanings.

In its captial form, V can stand for Victoria (QV); Viscount and Viscountess, Venerable, and the chemical element vanadium.

---

varn	varnish.
varsity	university.
VASARI	Visual Art System for Archiving and Retrieval of Images (computer term).
VAT	value added tax.
vb	verb (**vbl** = verbal).
VC	Victoria Cross, for valour and conspicuous bravery in wartime; Vatican City; Vice-Chancellor/Chairman.

VC10	Vickers-Armstrong series of aircraft.
VCC	Veteran Car Club of Great Britain.
VCR	video casette recorder (and player).
VD	venereal disease.
VDC	Volunteer Defence Corps.
VDH	valvular disease of the heart.
VDQS	*vins délimités de qualité supérieure* = French Ministry of Agriculture wine designation between *Appellation d'Origine Contrôlée* (**AC, AOC**) and *Vin de Pays* or table wine.
VDU	visual display unit.
VE Day	Victory in Europe Day, May 8, 1945.
veg	vegetable; vegetables; vegetarian.
veh	vehicle; vehicular.
Ven	Venerable; Venice; Venus; Venezuela.
ven	venomous; veneer.
ver	version; verify; verification; vermilion (also verm).
verb sap	*verbum satis sapienti* = a word is enough to the wise.
vern	vernacular.
verso	*reverso* = other side; in a book, the left-hand page.
vert	vertical; vertebra.
vet	veterinary surgeon; veteran.
VF	very fine (coins); very fair (weather); voice frequency.
vf band	voice-frequency band.
VFM	value for money.
vg	very good.
VGPI	visual glide path indicator.
vh	vertical height.
VHF	very high frequency (**UHF** = ultra high frequency); very high fidelity.

131

VHS	Video Home System (videotape standard).
VI	Virgin Islands; Vancouver Island, Canada.
viad	viaduct.
vib	vibration.
vic	vicinity; vicar; vicarage.
vign	vignette (*also* **vig**).
VIN	vehicle identification number.
VIP	very important person.
VIR	*Victoria Imperatrix Regina* = Victoria, Empress and Queen.
VJ Day	Victory over Japan and end of World War II, August 15, 1945.
Vlad	Vladivostock.
VLF	very low frequency.
VLR	very long range aircraft.
VMH	Victoria Medal of Honour (for horticulture).
VMS	Voluntary Medical Services medal.
V-neck	V-cut neck in clothing apparel.
VO	voice over (in broadcasting, film-making); Victorian Order; very old; veterinary/valuation officer.
voc	vocalist.

Protest Acronyms

Environmental organisations have become adept at grabbing attention by the clever, although sometimes laborious, use of initials: **nimby** (Not in my back yard) is a good example. Others, equally to the point, include the anti-dog lobby, **SCOOP** (*Stop Crapping On Our Property*); **GASP** (*Group Against Smog and Pollution*); and **STOP** (*Students Tired of Pollution*).

vocab	vocabulary.
vol	volume; voluntary; volatile; volcano.
VP	Vice-President; vanishing point; variable pitch.
VPL	visible panty line.
VR	*Victoria Regina* = Queen Victoria.
VRC	Victoria Racing Club, Melbourne.
V Rev	Very Reverend.
vs	versus = against (ie, England vs West Indies).
VSCC	Vintage Sports Car Club.
VSO	very superior old (designation for Cognac, Port etc.); also **VSOP** (very superior old pale).
Vte	*Vicomte* = French Viscount (*Vtesse* = Vicomtesse).
VTOHL	Vertical take-off, horizontal landing.
VTOL	vertical take-off and landing.
VTR	videotape recording.
vulg	vulgar (*also* **vul**).
VW	Volkswagen = literally, German people's car.

W

W	west; western; Wales; west postal district in London.
w	width; weight; win; won; woman; wife; warm; wet; wind; water; white; watt (electrical unit); week; waist; with; wide; wicket (in cricket).
WA	West Africa; Western Australia.

WAAA	Women's Amateur Athletic Association.
WAC	Women's Army Corps (US).
WACB	World Association for Christian Broadcasting.
WAE	when actually employed.
WAF	with all faults.
WAFFLE	wide angle fixed field locating equipment.
WAGGGS	World Association of Girl Guides and Girl Scouts.
wam	wife and mother.
w & t	wear and tear.
warn	warning.
warr	warranty.
WASP	white Anglo-Saxon Protestant.
WATS	Wide Area Telephone Service.
WB	Warner Brothers Pictures Inc; World Bank for Reconstruction and Development; water board.
wb	wheel base; wave band.
WBA	World Boxing Association (of America).
WBC	World Boxing Council.
WC	War cabinet; west–central postal district of London; workmens' compensation.
W/C	Wing Commander (*also* **W Cdr**).
wc	water closet; without charge; wheelchair.
WCC	War Crimes Commission; World Council of Churches.
WCEU	World Christian Endeavour Union.
WCF	World Congress of Faiths.
WCG	Worldwide Church of God.
WCT	World Championship Tennis.
WCTU	Women's Christian Temperance Union.
WCWB	World Council for the Welfare of the Blind.

WD	War Department; well developed (*also* **w/d**).
wdv	written-down value.
w/e	weekend.
WEA	Workers' Educational Association.
wea	weather; weapon.
Wed	Wednesday (*also* **We**; **Wednes**).
wef	with effect from.
wf	wrong font (typography).
WFA	Women's Football Association.
WFTU	World Federation of Trade Unions.
w/h	withholding.
WHA	World Hockey Association.
WHAM	Winning Hearts And Minds, a cynical propaganda campaign during the Vietnam War.
whf	wharf (*also* **wh**).
WHO	World Health Organisation.
whse	warehouse (*also* **whs**).
whsle	wholesale (*also* **whsl**).
WI	Women's Institute; West Indies; Windward Islands.
WIA	Wounded in action.
wid	widow; widower.
WIF	West Indies Federation.
WILCO	will comply.
Wilts	Wiltshire.
W Ind	West Indies.
Winn	Winnipeg, Canada.
WIP	work in progress.
WJC	World Jewish Congress.
wk	week; well known.
wkg	working (**wkr** = worker; **wks** = works).
wkly	weekly.
wkt	wicket (in cricket).
WL	water line; wavelength (*also* **w/l**); West Lothian.
wld	would.

wmk	watermark (in papermaking and philately).
WMO	World Meteorological Organisation.
wnl	within normal limits.
WNO	Welsh National Opera.
WNP	Welsh Nationalist Party.
WO	War Office; warrant/welfare officer; wireless operator.
w/o	without; written off.
wob	washed overboard.
wog	water, oil or gas; worker on government service (*also* **wogs**).
Wolves	Wolverhampton Wanderers Football Club.
WOMAN	World Organisation for Mothers of All Nations.
Women's Lib	Women's Liberation movement.
Wor	Worshipful.
Worcs	Worcestershire.
WOTCHA	wonderful old thing, considering his/her age.
wp	waste pipe; waste paper; working party.
WPA	Works Projects Administration (US); World Presbyterian Alliance.
wpb	wastepaper basket.
WPC	Woman Police Constable.
wpe	white porcelain enamel.
WPGA	Women's Professional Golfers' Association.
WPI	World Press Institute.
wpm	words per minute (typing, shorthand).
WRAAC	Women's Royal Australian Army Corps.
WRAAF	Women's Royal Australian Air Force.
WRAC	Women's Royal Army Corps.

WRAF	Women's Royal Air Force.
WRANS	Women's Royal Australian Naval Service.
WRNR	Women's Royal Naval Reserve.
WRNS	Women's Royal Naval Service, formerly **Wrens**.
WRU	Welsh Rugby Union; who are you? (telex message).
WRVS	Women's Royal Voluntary Service.
WSC	World Series Cricket.
WSCF	World Student Christian Federation.
WSJ	*Wall Street Journal* (US).
wsp	water supply point.
WT	withholding tax; watertight.
wt	weight.
W/T	wireless telegraphy.
WTO	World Tourism Organisation; Warsaw Treaty Organisation.
wtr	winter; writer.
WTUC	World Trade Union Conference.
w/v	weight to volume ratio; water valve (*also* **wv**).
WW1	1914–18 World War (**WW2** = 1939–45 World War).
WWF	World Wildlife Fund.
WWO	Wing Warrant Officer.
WWSU	World Water Ski Union.
ww	white wall (car tyres).
WWW	World Weather Watch; *Who Was Who* yearbooks.
wysiwyg	what you see is what you get.

X

X	Roman numeral for 10; location mark on maps; X Certificate for motion pictures to which under-16-year-olds may not be admitted; symbol for Cross eg **King's X**.
x	multiplied by; extra.
x'd	executed.
Xer	Xerox copier or reproduction.
XL	extra large.
Xmas	Christmas.
X-position	A position used in sexual intercourse described at some length in Dr Alex Comfort's *The Joy of Sex* but ultimately impossible to adequately illustrate.
x rd	crossroads.
xs	expenses.
Xth	tenth.
xtra	extra.
XX	double-strength ale (**XXX** = triple strenth; **XXXX** = quadruple strength, or 3.9% alcohol by weight); **XXXX** is also a euphemism for four-letter words.

Y

Y	yen, Japanese currency unit.
y	yard; year; young; yellow; yacht.
YA	young adults.
YAG	Yttrium-aluminium garnet = artificial diamond.
Y & R	Young and Rubicam, advertising agency.
YB	yearbook (*also* **yr b**; **yearb**).
YC	Young Conservative; Yale College (US); Yacht Club.
YD	Yugoslav dinar, currency unit.
yd	yard.
YEB	Yorkshire Electricity Board.
Yem	Yemen.
YES	Youth Employment Service.
YFC	Young Farmers' Club.
YFCU	Young Farmers' Club of Ulster.
YHA	Youth Hostels Association.
Yid	Yiddish; Yiddisher.
Yippie	Youth International Party member.
YMCA	Young Men's Christian Association.
YMCU	Young Men's Christian Union.
yo	year old (eg, **2yo** or **2-yo** = two-year-old in racing).
yob	year of birth; backward boy.
YOC	Young Ornithologists' Club of the **RSPB**.
yod	year of death.
yom	year of marriage.
Yorks	Yorkshire.
YPA	Young Pioneers of America.
yr	year; your (**yrs** = yours).
YRA	Yacht Racing Association.

YTS	Youth Training Scheme.
YTYTK	You're too young to know (From ITMA radio show).
Yuppie	young upwardly-mobile professional.
YWCA	Young Women's Christian Association.
YWCTU	Young Women's Christian Temperance Union.
YWS	Young Wales Society.

Z

Z, z	zero; zone; zenith.
Zag	Zagreb, Yugoslavia.
Zam	Zambia.
Zan	Zanzibar.
ZANU	Zimbabwe African National Union.

Zip

America's Zip Code (**Zip** = Zone Improvement Plan) was conceived in 1963 as 37,000 five-digit numbers, each representing a geographical area of the US, to facilitate mail sorting and delivery. It has now grown to a nine-digit, two-section number, eg, 48492–6127, which everyone has to attach to their address. Britain achieved the same result with a combination of six letters and numbers.

ZAPU	Zimbabwe African People's Union.
ZEBRA	zero-energy breeder-reactor assembly.
Zl	zloty, Polish currency unit.
Zoo	zoological gardens.
zool	zoology; zoological; zoologist.
Zur	Zurich, Switzerland.
zzz	sleep; snoozing.

A Full List of Titles Available from Mandarin in this series

While every effort is made to keep prices low, it is sometimes necessary to increase prices at short notice. Mandarin Paperbacks reserves the right to show new retail prices on covers which may differ from those previously advertised in the text or elsewhere.

The prices shown below were correct at the time of going to press.

All these books are available at your bookshop or newsagent, or can be ordered direct from the address below. Just tick the titles you want and fill in the form below.

Cash Sales Department, PO Box 5, Rushden, Northants NN10 6YX.

Please send cheque, payable to 'Reed Book Services Ltd.', or postal order for purchase price quoted and allow the following for postage and packing:

£1.00 for the first book, 50p for the second; **FREE POSTAGE AND PACKING FOR THREE BOOKS OR MORE PER ORDER.**

NAME (Block letters) ....

ADDRESS ....

....

☐ I enclose my remittance for ....

☐ I wish to pay by Access/Visa Card Number

Expiry Date